IF THE WORLD WAS A BANK IT HAD BEEN RESCUED

IF THE WORLD WAS A BANK IT HAD BEEN RESCUED

A NEW WORLD IS NOT POSSIBLE, A NEW ECONOMIC SYSTEM IS!

RALPH T. NIEMEYER

iUniverse, Inc.
NEW YORK   BLOOMINGTON

If the World was a Bank it had been rescued
A new World is not possible, a new economic system is!

Cover photo by Ralph T. Niemeyer © 2009

The photo shows a figurative statue featuring struggling human beings at the feet of
goddess Europa upholding the Euro-Symbol "€". The statue is situated at the main
entrance of the European Parliament's Paul-Henri Spaak-building in Brussels.

iUniverse books may be ordered through booksellers or by contacting:

iUniverse
1663 Liberty Drive
Bloomington, IN 47403
www.iuniverse.com
1-800-Authors (1-800-288-4677)

Because of the dynamic nature of the Internet, any Web addresses or links contained in this
book may have changed since publication and may no longer be valid.

ISBN: 978-1-4401-8068-2 (sc)
ISBN: 978-1-4401-8069-9 (dj)
ISBN: 978-1-4401-8075-0 (ebk)

Printed in the United States of America

iUniverse rev. date: 11/23/2009

CONTENTS

I.   Uncle Barack's Cabin 1

II.   A Debt-, not a Credit Crisis 23

III. The Anglo-American Virtual Reality Casino 41

IV. Methodological Insanity 79

V.   Someone *Made-off* 129

VI. The Great Depression – this time in Technicolor 149

VII. *Warshipping* the scapegoat 159

VIII. If God asked whether you're good for a loan, were
      you?! 183

To

Sahra, my all-above loved wife and all people who share her ideals…

In Socialism, the banks are first nationalised and then ruined, in Capitalism they are first ruined and then nationalised.

Angela Merkel,
German chancellor

MOST OPINIONS ARE
INTEREST-DRIVEN

It is not only a question of being allowed a different opinion but not seldom it is a matter of having different interests that may feed one's opinion. It is vital to establish who is expressing what 'opinion' and what the underlying interest may be.

In case of Cuba one could say that one potential feeder of opinions that differ from the Cuban communist mainstream can be aligned with interests in regaining control of parts of the economy by for instance re-privatising banana plants or opening casinos for rich American tourists.

In case of the EU it has become clear that to be pro European in fact means to be pro Lisbon-Treaty which unfortunately implies to be forced to swallow one neo-liberal pill after the other, accept militarization and wage-, standard- and tax-dumping, but if one doesn't get it down the throat one becomes subject to be labelled anti-European or even 'nationalistic' by the pro European side. This may illustrate that no opinion is expressed in this debate being truly honest and free of interests.

Just because human beings tend to hold monologues rather than exchanging opinions in a debate or democratic discourse it can be deemed logic that never a dialogue of opinions free of interests can take place. The aim of this book rather is to contribute to the debate by showing naked facts while dismantling ideologies that are used to cover up underlying interests by 'opinion leaders' who actually only serve a certain interest. This does imply colleagues from all kind of media in particular as well.

RTN

THE 'BAD BANK' – PRINCIPLE

Amid social unrest spreading that followed the collapse of our economic system our leaders were eager to fight the symptoms by stimulus packages and 'bad banks', by tax incentives and by easing accountancy standards.

None of the above remedies will work. The financial capitalistic model is as dead as the East European Socialism in 1989 has been. Like 20 years ago there are some ideologists who do not understand that their time was up and that the rest of us were moving on.

The capitalistic system can not be fixed. One can, of course, prolong it's decline and make it more painful for everyone.

It is like an avalanche of stones and rocks going downhill. A clever leader would not try to stem against the rock from underneath it but would rather step aside and give it a kick so that it goes down quicker and in a straight way causing as little damage as possible after which one could start to rebuild society and establish a sound economic model.

But, what President Obama and many other leaders are up to is to check the seatbelts and to cling onto the handbrakes while we are driven over the cliff. The absurdity comes to a climax when one imagines someone to find any kind of a safe place inside that particular vehicle.

Not long ago, I came across the following little story a colleague told me:

It is August. In a small town on the South Coast of France, holiday season is in full swing, but it is raining so there is not too much business happening. Everyone is heavily in debt.

Luckily, a rich Russian tourist arrives in the foyer of the small local hotel. He asks for a room and puts a 100 Euro note on the reception counter, takes a key and goes to inspect the room located up the stairs on the third floor.

The hotel owner takes the banknote in hurry and rushes to his meat supplier to whom he owes 100 Euros.

The butcher takes the money and races to his supplier to pay his debt. The wholesaler rushes to the farmer to pay 100 Euros for pigs he purchased some time ago.

The farmer triumphantly gives the 100 Euro note to a local prostitute who gave him her services on credit.

The prostitute goes quickly to the hotel, as she owed the hotel 100 Euros for her hourly room use to entertain clients.

At that moment, the rich Russian is coming down to reception and informs the hotel owner that the proposed room is unsatisfactory and takes his 100 Euros back and departs.

There was neither any profit nor any income. But everyone no longer had any debt and the small town people looked optimistically towards their future. Could this be the solution to the global financial crisis, or is there a catch here?

Closer scrutiny reveals why 'Bad Bank' is not a solution at all. In the theory underlying this short story the Russian tourist would be the state. But, the state would, other than the Russian tourist, never demand his money back.

Too much depends on how long the Russian guest needs to decide whether he likes to stay in the room or not and if so, for how long.

That's how the theory would go. The economy would be kept going by the state taking on the bad debt. But in real life it doesn't stop with the Russian tourist coming down the stairs and not demanding his money back. In real life, the state would not be the Russian tourist. The story would rather be as follows:

The banker in the local branch of the country's major bank who had intercepted the money by promising the hotel owner an astronomical return on investment for the 100 € the hotel owner had received back from the prostitute, covered only the losses he had made with previous speculations.

Now, as the Russian tourist comes down the stairs demanding the 100 € deposit back, the hotel owner only shrugs his shoulders and writes a bad check hoping that the Russian tourist won't have time to go to the cashier's desk as it was closed for a long lunch break leaving the impatient Russian tourist with no option but to post the check for collection when he is back at home in Moscow.

This can take for ages, but ultimately the check will hit the account and the hotel owner, if he is still not in funds because the local banker has still not doubled his investment citing a 'bad market', defaults the check might already pack his bags to go to prison or the Russian tourist might generously forget about the 100 € and move on with his life prompting the banker to think the system should be patented as it was kind of re-inventing the license for printing money. For his continued gambling the banker would look forward to more indecisive Russian tourists to come and visit the town even if they decide not to stay in the hotel and consume nothing.

In the real world, the state would neither bail out the hotel owner nor the Russian tourist but the banker.

Transferred to the global crisis this should not mean that we all go to prostitutes but rather to eliminate all debt since it is the debt-bubble that is hanging over us like the sword of Damocles.

Debit on one side of the balance sheet means Credit on the other side. Someone holds all those debts and wants to present those sooner or later at the cashier's desk. Usually, those who own debts have become rich through theft, gambling or speculation, not hard work. A few exceptions only prove this rule to be right.

Now, as the party comes to an end the butler is asked to pay for it. Literally, one could say, that those who had 2-3% annual pay-increase if they were lucky, are now rescuing those who only made 40% or a bit less when they had a bad year.

Those banks (and their shareholders) who lent ridiculous amounts to mortgage-borrowers who were seeking to finance their over-priced family homes made fortunes over the years and traded such debts although they knew it would turn soar one day.

The over-indebtedness the capitalistic economy created trillion-fold by handing out loans and credit cards secured by mortgages instead of allowing the working population to participate in economic booms by fair wage increases had led into an absolutely foreseeable disaster.

Now the banks and their shareholders are in difficulties because their system of debt-financed profit maximization became unreal.

One cold say, the assassin mutated into a suicide-bomber who is being rescued by his victims and rushed to the emergency room.

And, as the patient is on life support machines remedy is sought in nationalization but the patient hallucinates of the privatization of the nation-state once he sprung from the devil's shuffle.

That's why we are hardly in a credit crisis but rather a DEBT CRISIS.

Those institutional investors, banks as well as rich private individuals who by creating debt bubbles by means of hedging and trading of otherwise useless financial instruments are about to drive us over the cliff, should come to terms with the fact that the debts won't be paid back ever.

Not today and not in a generation's time. It will be painful for all those who hold the debt titles but they will recover from the shock one day. The have made hundreds of per cent in the years before and can afford the loss of future earnings.

Let's not start with a *Socialism of the Billionaires* by cutting back on the poor, sick and old, by denying our children good education, a peaceful world and ecologic society, and by cementing a dreadful mechanism of debt-bubble building based on an unjust distribution of wealth from bottom to top of society..

Elimination of debt inevitably results in repossession of wealth accumulated by creating bubbles. The owners and shareholders of investment banks, hedge funds and private equity firms won't like that idea but who says they will be asked for their opinion?

The 'Bad-Bank' - principle instead must have been invented in a nightclub!

It has been particularly invented by those who benefit from it as it allows the same hedge fund junkies and private equity sharks to start anew by the public supplying them with fresh liquidity while eating their bad debts.

Let's just tell the owners of big debt to write it off and let's start from scratch. Not only is it fair, it also is the only workable scenario to get our economies back on track and avoid wars, civil wars, bloodshed and revolutions.

20 years ago, when the Eastern European Socialism collapsed over *billion*-fold deficits, word was on the street that Capitalism finally has

won over Socialism, but from today's perspective it rather only seems to have outlasted it forcing it's beneficiaries to write of *trillions*.

My generation remembers well how the collapsing Socialism had been dictated the conditions for it's surrendering and it comes with a bitter taste to see the financial Capitalism now dictate it's saviours the conditions for it's decline and resurrection.

Socialism is seen by many these days as being dead, but who knows, maybe it only pretends?! But, likewise, Capitalism more and more frequently pretends to be dead either. It could be prudent to think of a third way. Our real economy was in good shape when the 'Credit' crunch happened!

Ralph T. Niemeyer
Two years after August 11th(2007), one year after September 14th (2008)

I.

UNCLE BARACK'S CABIN

Uncle Barack's Cabin

February 2009

The situation President Barack Obama found on 20th January 2009 when he took seat in the Oval Office couldn't be worse:

The US trade balance speaks for itself, but it doesn't speak for the US's economic wisdom in leading the world. Since Ronald Reagan by his high-interest policy in fact de-industrialised the US there is not much left the US still produces.

During the two terms of the Bush administration military 'goods' one shouldn't want to buy and Microsoft software which only dominates the world market because of a classical monopoly position became the back-bone of the US economy.

And, the US exported all kinds of worthless toilet paper in form of stocks, bonds, shares and 'asset backed securities'. The latter were used to finance American standard of living but this could only work on basis of the *Ponzi*-pyramid-scheme or chain - letter system every school kid knows sooner or later reaches its limits.

There would be a lot that needed to be changed by the new president, but is President Barack Obama ready for that, one may ask, and if so, would the powers to be let him?

It has become clear, that Wall Street understood that the president has to apply some Keynesianism in order to keep the show on the road.

Ralph T. Niemeyer

WALL STREET HAD PLANNED WITHOUT RODHAM CLINTON & McCAIN

Senator McCain would not have done anything different either, one can imagine as the new administration has hardly been left with any choice.

But, what will happen when it comes to not only administrating the decline but to some real changes required to bring the American economy (the real one, not the bubble-builders and chain letter fetishists, please!) back on track and make God's Own Country a leader in industrial innovation again? Is Barack Obama ready for that fight against the Hedge Fund – junkies and Private Equity - pirates?

The German Focus-Money magazine instead pointed out what the donors of the new president expect: "What does the change Barack Obama is promising mean for the stock markets? His program of healthcare, education and alternative energy will let stocks of companies which are involved in those fields rise."[1]

According to this article Barack Obama's presidential campaign had received three times of the financial institution's donations compared to the campaign of Senator McCain. Goldman Sachs supported the Democrat's campaign by 605,980 Dollars, JP Morgan with 403,407 Dollars, UBS with 370,130 Dollars and Citigroup with 363,454 Dollars. The Republican opponent only received 225,260 Dollars from Merrill Lynch, 209,951 Dollars from Citigroup, 166,387 Dollars from the international law firm Greenberg Traurig and 164,205 Dollars from the telephone company AT&T.

These figures illustrate that Wall Street had a clear preference. These investment bankers may have hoped that like in November 1928 when Calvin Coolidge won the presidency amid financial turmoil a "victory boom" can be ignited and let the markets go up again.

---

1   Focus Money Nr. 26 18 June 2008

CREATING BUBBLES, NOW IN HEALTH CARE, EDUCATION, GREEN ENERGY

And, indeed, room for initiating several bubbles was plenty in President Obama's program: United Health Group will be the greatest beneficiary of the planned state-sponsored health program. The company is the largest health insurer in the U.S. counting 73 million clients.

Together with the U.S. government United Health Group operates *AmeriChoice* which is designed to serve low income households. The Obama team says they will give 47 million uninsured Americans access to doctors, specialists and clinics.

JP Morgan predicted a 25% rise of the stocks of this company.

This is all fine as long as not a 'Health Care – Bubble' is created which will force hospitals to cut down on spending for patient's health in compliance with shareholder's expectations as we have seen in Germany recently.

The second big hype of the Obama-presidency was already there before him: Alternative Energy. Not only the talk about Climate Change we all got bugged with by EU Commission president José Manuel Barroso and Nobel Peace Prize bearer Albert Gore is the reason for the clean energy hype.

The US who imports oil of the value of 41 million Dollars per hour could certainly benefit from exploring alternatives. The only question once more is: is it feasible to put more funds behind it? "Alternative Energy market is already awash with money" leading newspapers titled more than a year ago[2]. If more money than necessary is injected into companies it will create a bubble.

Barack Obama has cited the US's dependence on oil as one of the biggest problems and he is determined to tackle that. That sounds like if a lone fighter is standing up against all these powerful energy multinationals. The fact that these were only half heartedly supporting Mr McCain shows that they became already friendly with Mr Obama: sure, all of the oil companies already are involved in alternative energy exploration and production.

---

2 The Guardian 27th September 2007

OBAMA KNOWS HOW TO PLEASE SHAREHOLDERS

The shareholders of Exxon, Texaco and Chevron aren't interested in how the return is made, be it from oil, gas, wind or sun. They even were cynical enough to eat the profits from bio-fuel although this led to starvation in the so called "Third World".

Well before the peak of the financial crisis Focus-Money magazine titled: "The Safest Bet of this Century: *Agrar*-stocks" and quite openly described in those articles how bio-fuel increases the demand for agricultural products. The biggest US wind turbine - company, Florida Power and Light, as well as General Electric (GE) look forward to the new boom.

But nobody seems to be as encouraged by Barack Obama's vision as the solar technology companies. Altogether, some 700 million Dollars had been donated in the election campaign by First Solar, Sun Power and Evergreen, three quarters of it to Mr Obama's campaign. Shares of these companies are already on the rise. Since the beginning of the Climate Change – hype in January 2007, stocks of First Solar had gained eight times of its value.

Last but not least, the education offensive of the new US government also promises to pay off. Barrack Obama's proposed tax cuts will directly bolster private universities, colleges and private schools. The education market is extremely hot as dozens of stock market listed companies such as Apollo Group, Career Education Corp., Corinthean College or Strayer Education and Devry report already sharp increases of student registrations. Stocks of ITT Educational Services as well as those of Devry within only 50 days tripled their value.

Neither at that time presidential contesters Senator Hillary Rodham Clinton nor Senator John McCain had understood that the people behind Wall Street, the owners, the *tigers*, had already planned without them as none of them have that Messiah-like aura.

Instead, shareholders not only became comfortable with Barack Obama but they understood that they need someone who can please the masses in the worst time of the economic crisis that is yet to come.

But, Mr. Obama has to see that he is not too much associated with those Ultra High Net-Worth Individuals (as Merrill Lynch classifies them) who want to use him as kind of a Messiah calming down the masses while they continue to uphold an unsustainable economic model that may lead into a catastrophe prompting the president to declare wars on a worldwide level while putting God's Own Country under martial law in order to prevent it from breaking up and going under in unrest and riots.

OBAMA'S PLAN A NOT A PLAN B FOR EUROPE

June 2009

Never has there been such a great deal of confusion among mainstream economists how to classify inflation, as a threat or a last resort to recover. But, it is also difficult to identify these days who is considered a neo-liberal hardliner and who a Keynesian leftist economist. The latter usually decry inflation as "reactionary deprivation" while mainstream economists these days applaud President Obama printing trillions and defy ECB President Trichet's cautious interest cuts although their camp usually would demand exactly that: to avoid inflation at whatever it takes to prevent the assets of the rich from becoming devalued. What is it that makes experienced economists switch sides both ways?

Reason for such widespread uncertainty is the escalating public debt in the US and the Obama-administration's creative monetary policy. Since the Federal Reserve had reached the bottom of the barrel at 0% base rate traditional interest rate policy has become history. Usually, central banks are channelling liquidity into the banking system by so called Repo-transactions. Banks have to deposit certain commercial paper as collateral with the central bank in order to obtain cash for a fixed interest rate for a certain time. It is then up to them to decide at what rate such loans will be passed on. In any case, these papers have to be bought back by the bank from the central bank after the time period previously agreed on.

This is where the trouble started. The banks couldn't get rid off their dubious papers and therefore didn't pass on the cheap cash they got from the central bank. Logically, the credit conditions for companies and households in the US dramatically worsened as long-term interest rates were rising despite the zero-percent interest rate of the FED.

The dilemma shall be solved by the so called "quantitative easing" that had already been explored by the Japanese central bank in the 1990ies. Quantitative easing means that a central bank buys up shares and commercial papers and by this creates an artificial demand leading to a lowering of interest rates and easing of credit conditions for such companies. Other than in the traditional scenario the central bank not only influences the short term but also long term interest rates. In case the shares and commercial papers bought by the central bank are "toxic" the risk is born by the state and by this the taxpayer.

ECB IS MORE CAUTIOUS, BUT FOR HOW LONG?

So far, the European Central Bank (ECB) rejects quantitative easing outright but not so the Federal Reserve. Chairman Ben Bernanke announced to buy shares and papers worth more than a trillion Dollars (a thousand billions!), most of it collateralised mortgage bonds, in other words exactly those "toxic" papers which triggered the credit crisis on August 11, 2007, and 300 billions of US treasury bonds. The latter wouldn't pose the risk that Uncle Sam was left with worthless toilet paper but nevertheless the direct financing of state debts by printing money is regarded as one of the deadly sins mainstream economists would outright reject as it leads to escalating inflation.

It would be wrong to brand those who warn of Dollar-inflation as 'neo-liberals' although the usual mantra accompanying demands for higher interest rates, fiscal austerity, wage moderation and social cuts is about the dangers of inflation. But, not all criticism of the current Dollar-inflation can be put down to neo-liberals being eager to protect their clientele's assets. On the other hand, not all who warn of deflation these days and propagate 'quantitative easing' are not automatically to be seen as progressive. The European industrial association 'Business Europe' for instance has urged the European Central Bank to follow the Federal Reserve in buying up shares and toxic assets which would of course mean to have the taxpayer step in if things go wrong while in the positive case the profits still would be earned by the private owners. And, many bankers are, of course, in favour of quantitative easing if only the central bank bought up their worthless commercial papers, "asset backed securities (ABS)", "mortgage backed securities (RMBS)" or derivatives. Luckily, so far ECB President Jean-Claude Trichet resisted following any such proposals.

CHINA'S ANXIETY OVER US' HYPER-INFLATION

China, as it holds 2 trillion in currency reserves, most of it in Dollars and 740 billion of which in US treasury bonds, is taking a dim view on the Obama-administration's money printing reflexes. Chinese Prime Minister Wen Jiabao made it clear: "We lent the US a huge amount of money and we are extremely worried. The US government should watch its credit worthiness, fulfil its obligations and guarantee Chinese assets."

Logically, China can not simply change its Dollar reserves into any other currency without provoking what it actually wants to avoid: a rapid devaluation of the US currency. In other words, the turbo-capitalistic Socialism of China inadvertently rescues the socialistic Capitalism of the United States.

But, does printing money really directly result in inflation? Or are the Chinese simply paranoid and is Ben Bernanke right in arguing that in lieu of the crisis the FED's strategy is the only way to prevent the economy from entering a dreadful depression-deflation – spiral? Indeed, it doesn't look like inflation so far. Prices in the Euro-zone had increased by 3.3% throughout 2008 but since January 2009 it is 0.5%, bordering deflation. Spain is the first Euro-zone member state to officially report a negative inflation. Germany reported in mid April a 0.1% drop in consumer prices from March for the first time since 1999. Also the US consumption indices rather suggest deflation.

This shouldn't come as a surprise as in the last quarter of 2008 growth in both, the US as well as the Euro-zone plummeted by 6%, in Japan it was the double of it. Industrial orders in the Euro-zone had dropped by 34.2% between January 2008 and January 2009. More than 4.5 million people lost their jobs in the US since beginning of the crisis. There is no hope that anything will change, soon. The OECD expects a drop in GDP of 4 % in both, US and Euro-zone in 2009 and an additional 25 million unemployed in all industrialised countries (double of what it was in 2007).

NOT A GOOD EXAMPLE, BUT AN EXAMPLE: JAPAN

Isn't it ludicrous to assume there could be any inflation in such an economic environment? It is true: a massively expanded monetary emission of the central bank doesn't necessarily lead to price increases. Also Japan had, in order to fight permanent depression and deflation, printed vast amounts of cash in the 1990ies and today still records inflation at around 0%. The most decisive question is who receives the extra cash and for what it is spent. Only, if the money ever reaches those who actually want to buy bred or electronic goods or a car, in other words, once it reaches the man in the street and by this the goods market of the real economy and only when it creates a suddenly increasing demand on that market, will it lead to demand-related inflation.

So who receives the trillions worth in presents from the FED? FED chairman Ben Shalom Bernanke's quantitative easing – strategy will flood the dried up arteries of financial institutions, banks, mortgage lenders and hedge funds. He calculates that these will use their newly re-gained liquidity on the financial markets. If, for instance, they buy stocks and shares on the secondary market this will increase the value of those having the effect of making the emissions of shares for companies cheaper as well. It is also intended to jump-start the mortgage market and to lower interest rates for such.

PLACEBO-EFFECT FOR REAL ECONOMY AND CONSUMERS

And, indeed, the long term interest rates for 30-year mortgages dropped from 5.15% to 5.09% after the FED's announcement. Only to that extent which the FED expands the credit volume for businesses and consumers and provide for lower interest rates will the new liquidity stream from the FED have any effect on demand. So, this is only affecting a fraction of the newly printed money. Likewise won't the buying-up of US treasury bonds have a real effect on domestic demand. Also the escalating US state deficit only marginally is owed to an increased expenditure. The bulk of the rescuing measurements applied by the government are directed at rotten banks and insurance companies. The vast majority of funds provided by the FED is designed to allow the management to fiddle the balance sheets, recapitalise, paying creditors (usually other financial institutions) and thus will stay within the speculative financial circles.

Even if some of the money is paid in form of bonuses, interest or dividends to private individuals it will in most cases simply be saved again and not consumed as all previous savings rate statistics suggest. The upper quintile doesn't eat, drink, travel, consume significantly more when being dropped an additional bag of money into their lap. US finance secretary Timothy Franz Geithner's program to provide a trillion Dollars in order to encourage hedge funds to speculate in otherwise un-sellable toxic commercial paper while have Uncle Sam carry the entire risk just matches the FED's policy. Master of all bubble-building, Alan Greenspan, just recently praised the Ponzi-schemes of this world again and predicted a swift recovery. He didn't specify, of course, which economy, the bubbles, or the real economy, he referred to, so there will be another hype before the final crash, and maybe another one or a few more.

But, even if the FED took over the financing of these trillions directly no cent of this additional cash would be spent in any supermarket as only the next speculation bubble will be fuelled. Maybe a few segments in the luxury goods sector might rebound as the US financial aristocracy will, for a brief moment, recover.

PERPETUUM MOBILE FOR HEDGE FUND JUNKIES & PRIVATE EQUITY SHARKS

In theory, a perpetual mobile in which the central bank endlessly prints money which almost exclusively ends up on the casino tables of the financial markets creating bubbles over bubbles is possible. And, at present all signs are pointing into that direction if one scrutinises Washington's 'plan A'. President Obama seems to be poised to revitalise the bubble economy at whatever it takes.

But, one may ask, why the money that is used for such insane speculation is not replaced by tokens? At least the negative effects for the real economy, consumer and taxpayer could be avoided in a way that ordinary citizens are not affected by some casino junkies in the Las Vegas' and Monte Carlo's of this world. It brought the world economy down that the virtual reality casino of the private equity sharks and hedge fund junkies had been allowed to use real money which ordinary citizens are now asked to pay back cent by cent.

Obama's 'plan A' could, for a few moments in history lead to a recovery of the real economy as booming financial markets as well as the income of the American upper class and better credit conditions for the vast majority of citizens might result from same but certainly not in a way that it sparks the threat of inflation. In fact, the US are obviously poised to try to let exactly that model of credit financed consumption celebrate a revival that has carried their and our European and world economy over the past decades.

OBAMA'S STRATEGY DOESN'T DIFFER FROM MADOFF'S SCHEME

To think that this model is to be continued seems to be ludicrous in lieu of the 42 trillion Dollars of debts of the American private sector, but on the one hand some of those debts are now taken over by Uncle Sam while on the other hand there is no objective upper limit to piling up debts. As long as enough liquidity (even if it is on credit basis) flows and covers not only the principal but also at least a part of the interest payments this game can continue into perpetuity. Like in the Bernard

Madoff – scandal, such a Ponzi-scheme will only collapse if the fresh influx of capital is interrupted for whatever reason, be it that like in Mr Madoff's case that the last stupid investor was found and there were no new ones coming after him, or like in case of the US that foreign investors and states mistrust the whole snowball system and escape into other currencies like let's say the Euro.

To cut a long story short: President Obama's 'plan A' is to have the state take over the otherwise simply bankrupt financial sector while financing the purchase of these toxic assets by letting national debt skyrocket as it is clear that the American taxpayer will never be able to pay for such a deficit. The Federal Reserve guarantees by its buying-up of shares a low long-term interest rate while eliminating the toxic jungle by buying bad debts from the financial institutions. The trillion fold FED-liquidity might get the credit-machinery back on track and let bonds, stocks and shares rise again. Banks, central banks throughout the world and international investors may regain their conviction of the American productivity miracle and queue-up to dump their money once more in the black hole of the US' debt-spiral.

It is hard to tell whether the Obama-administration believes in their 'plan A'. Today's financial markets have shown so far that anything is possible and the Americans are doing everything to cushion foreign investors otherwise they hadn't paid 50 billion Dollars of taxpayer's money in order to cover AIG's obligations towards foreign banks like Deutsche Bank AG (12 billion Dollars).

DEUTSCHE BANK AG INDIRECTLY BENEFITS FROM STATE-INTERVENTION

Funnily, Deutsche Bank AG – CEO Josef Ackermann pretends until today that his financial institution is doing well and doesn't require any state-aid thus luring at a 25% operational profit for 2009 again. But, it only appears to be logic seen from Mr. Ackermann's point of view as he managed to convince Christian-conservative German chancellor Angela Merkel and her Social-Democratic finance minister Peer Steinbrück to wait with their rescue mission for Hypo Real Estate (HRE) of which Deutsche Bank AG held billions worth of some sort of obligations until the guarantee of the Italian owner of HRE, Uni Credito, had expired. Hypo Real Estate (HRE) had been kind of the 'bad bank' for Hypo Vereinsbank which had participated in some dubious bubble scheme. Years before the credit crunch, HRE had in a complicated surgery being separated from Hypo Vereinsbank the latter which has been taken over by the Italian conglomerate of Uni Credito. Under these conditions Uni Credito had guaranteed HRE which also re-assured Deutsche Bank AG that the debt it held was kind of safe. As a courtesy to the Italian bankers the generous German government officials waited until the 5 year guarantee of Uni Credito for HRE expired. On the next morning in late September 2008 Mr. Ackermann called upon the German government to rescue Hypo Real Estate as it was "systematically relevant" as he called the bank. Logic, he did not want to see his bank's billion-fold debt obligations vanish. Indirectly, the tax payer has by rescuing HRE also saved Deutsche Bank AG or at least secured it's shareholders the next 25% return. Now, a special parliamentary investigation committee initiated by Germany's leftist former East-German socialist party *DIE LINKE* scrutinises in the German Bundestag who exactly planted the HRE rescue-coup and why one had waited to raise the red flags a day after the guarantee by Uni Credito had expired by this putting a huge burden onto the taxpayer's shoulders.

OBAMA'S PLAN B: NOT 'MADOFF', BUT RATHER 'MADE-OFF'

A different scenario is also possible if one takes into account that emissions worth three trillion Dollars are planned by the FED in 2009 alone: if the bigger and more sophisticated market participants do not see the FED's offerings as a signal to re-enter their scheme but rather as an opportunity to get rid off their Dollar papers without facing any losses and to make off and by this create a run out of the Dollar which would be enhanced by every new liquidity injection by the FED. Smaller countries suffer from such run out of their currency immediately if their central bank prints endlessly money. The result in those cases always is – provided there are no barriers for capital movements and currency exchange controls – inflation. If the outer value of a currency collapses imports will become extremely expensive regardless of actual demand. By importing intermediary goods and raw materials or energy the domestic production becomes more expensive as well and sets the classical spiral of depression and hyperinflation into motion. Countries in the so called "third world" know this best. It is terrible for such countries that they are forced to have their foreign debt in Dollars increasing the weight of the debt by the devaluation of the own currency. That's why smaller countries have to avoid such a scenario by whatever means. For the US this poses not as much of a problem as they are able to inflate-away their domestic as well as their foreign debt. One may suspect that President Obama keeps this scenario as a 'plan B' in the drawer should his 'plan A' prove illusory.

Winners and Losers

Indeed, an inflation of the Dollar would carry a few disadvantages but many advantages for the American upper-class. The most important advantage would be that the American economy would get rid off all its debt and could start from scratch. The disadvantage would be that because of such deliberate depreciation of the Dollar it could cost it its 'global reserve' status. A good deal of the American banking system's profit would be at stake. Nevertheless, it is unlikely that the Dollar doesn't play some kind of role as reserve and investment currency in the future as the American economy simply is too big to become totally insignificant. Another disadvantage would be, of course, that the American upper class would loose a part of its wealth but the damage would be relatively marginal as the ultra-rich in the US hold their portfolio in various currencies, also the Euro which probably won't be affected by the Dollar devaluation. Resistant to any inflation instead are any forms of real estate, shares and ownership of producing capacities. The latter could, as long as it is manufacturing industries, produce a higher return on investment again because a devaluing Dollar would make it possible to export goods and even conquer markets.

Ralph T. Niemeyer

DRIVING OVER THE CLIFF

Losers of such massive Dollar inflation would be the American middle class being deprived of the vast majority of their savings and pensions. Among those who would suffer if 'plan B' came into effect would also be emerging economies and developing countries which had, under the pressure of the currency regime of the past decades, starved billions of Dollar-reserves out of their populations. It has become clear during the South East Asian crisis in the late nineties that in a system of freely floating currency exchange only those central banks can defend their currency against speculative attacks which hold sufficient foreign reserves. As a result the Dollar reserves of emerging and developing countries had risen between 2000 and 2008 by 5.3 trillion Dollars. The vast majority of the huge US trade deficits of recent years have been financed by the central banks in those countries. In addition to China, which holds 2 trillion Dollars in reserves, the former South East Asian 'Tiger' states Singapore, Thailand, Malaysia and South Korea have increased their Dollar reserves drastically. But also Russia holds 376 billion Dollars, Brazil 203 billion, Mexico some 80 billion and even relatively poor countries like Turkey and Poland have bunkered some 70 billion Dollars. The majority is held in US treasury bonds.[3] More than half of the currently existing 6 trillion US treasury bonds are held by foreign entities. The idea to inflate-away its foreign debt may be enticing for Uncle Sam especially because the majority of the victims of such a crash – strategy are abroad. For the US this would only be a logic move as it matches its policy towards developing countries for the past decades. The fact that in addition to the developing countries some international financial institutions and a few ultra rich individuals are driven over the cliff wouldn't really bother President Obama, as the aforementioned would have had it in their hands to avoid 'plan B' to come into effect by continuing to buy American bonds and by this to save the house of cards from falling apart. It is like in case of a bank granting loans to a heavily over-indebted customer whose bankruptcy would inadvertently lead to the collapse of the lending institution

---

3 Financial Times Deutschland 20th/24th/30th March 2009
   Financial Times 8th March 2009
   Handelsblatt 25th June 2007

itself. But one day, the game is over. Other than said over-indebted customer the US upper class in a similar case is in the possession of a golden parachute: inflating the own currency by this making it obsolete to be held responsible for its own bankruptcy. That is their master strategy and President Obama seems to be willing to walk all 12 miles with them. One may, of course, debate the question of what use an economic system that is based on tins of hot air, chain letter –and snow-ball systems in real terms is.

Or one could simply pay people fair wages and social subsistence based on rise of productivity instead of trying to secure domestic demand and export by endlessly increasing debts.

AUGUR'S STABLE: BLUFFS AND SWINDLES EVERYWHERE

President Barack Obama, it has been said by many columnists, is facing times as tough as during the presidencies of Abraham Lincoln and Franklin D. Roosevelt. Meanwhile EU Commission and EU Council get ready to present their reform package in Washington. Although EU Council president Nicolas Sarkozy and IMF president Dominique Strauss-Kahn in classical state-interventionist style proposed reforms ringing hollow in the ears of any neo-classicist these new regulations are systematically rebuked.

Washington won't surrender control over the financial airspace of the US to any international body. At least, that's not what Barack Obama has been elected for. On the other hand, the Frenchmen's proposals as illusory they may be would be quite useless as long as the key elements of our system are becoming subject to reform as well. Like the Americans we in Europe have been marching down the wrong ally.

FROM CLINTON TO OBAMA: CREATIVE ACCOUNTING AND MANIPULATIONS

The creative way of financing of producing industries these days may suggest that even the real economy participates in the fictitious accumulation of wealth. Not necessarily does a rising turn-over in the

17

manufacturing industries mean that more goods have been produced and by this the share of disposable wealth of a society. By (legally) manipulating balance sheets and accounts one can virtually show or hide profits depending whether these are addressed to the revenue commission or the shareholders.

Credit-financed payments of dividends Private Equity Pirates often demand allows a company to distribute wealth which has not been produced yet. A modern way for hiding these payments can be seen in derivatives. Like Enron had transferred its expected future gains from gas and electricity sales into present times by derivatives many stock market listed companies did and still do so.

Analysts and rating agencies gout such strategies of increased shareholder value by directing more and more funds to such golden lambs. The company instead is confronted with two major problems: it is in serious danger if the expected (and already paid-out) returns can not be realised in an economic downturn.

Many industries probably could survive the present crisis if these companies had not been forced by Hedge Funds and Private Equity firms to issue derivatives. The second problem is that those gains that already have been paid out can't be paid out again. This creates tremendous pressure for the company to inherently increase profit and return on investment at whatever cost.

This system is quite limited. In order to keep the economic system of ever increasing profit rates alive creative accounting standards were introduced.

Barroso – Commission copied US model of hedonic pricing

An alternative way of making markets and investors believe that there are growth rates when in fact there is stagnation or even recession has been brought to perfection by the US and copied by the EU under the Barroso-Commission.

The so called hedonic pricing allows in statistics to apply 'quality adjustments' to miraculously show growth rates for instance in the car industry by assuming that because cars built nowadays contain features and improvements which are recorded as growth although today less cars than in the 1950ies are sold.

Since its beginning modern economic statistics would record prices on nominal basis on the one hand and in deflated manner on the other hand. This is the only way to be able to compare prices realistically.

If, for instance, an economy grows by 10% in a year it may stand for a magnificent boom or a deep depression. The only question is whether 10% more goods are sold or whether everything simply got 10% more expensive.

And, if inflation is around 2% but economic growth around 10% the overall economy is in perfect shape. But, if prices rose by 15% said nominal growth of 10% stands for a disastrous recession. Also wage increases of 10% in times of stable prices would be something different than during times of galloping inflation.

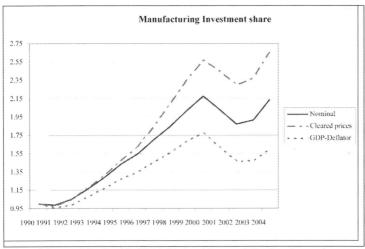

Source of data used for Graphic: NIPA (National Income & Product Account)

Since the early 1990ies an ever greater disparity between nominal and cleared prices can be noticed leaving the GDP deflator well behind. Hedonic pricing in the US showed growth rates during the Clinton-Gore administration although not more PCs were sold during the dotcom-boom but technology with better processors.

As most products over time improve their quality this system quite elegantly let's inflated prices disappear. Because increasing prices go in line with an increase of turn-over the latter appears as if there was an increase in consumption whereas in reality there is none.

It is a methodological question and it should be solved immediately as all those growth rates and inflation statistics are useless and even dangerous as no economist can verify what kind of development our economies in reality are taking.

Real change would start right here. One should not forget that the Eastern European Socialism collapsed 20 years ago because the system was no longer sustainable despite state controlled propaganda throwing sand into the eyes of the citizens.

The credibility of the advocates of a system in decline is minimal. Sarkozy, Berlusconi, and Merkel until recently stood on the other side calling for deregulation, liberalisation, and privatisation. And, by employing former Clinton-aides President Barack Obama indicated that he was not in for real change. It takes more than one brave president to clean out Augur's stable. Unless fundamentals are re-thought G20 leaders can save time and energy to travel to meet another as nothing will come out of such meetings unless the European Central Bank (ECB) agrees to stabilize the Dollar. This, of course, would mean inflation in the Euro-zone, but the alternative would inevitably bring down the Dollar to may be 20 cents towards the Euro, bearing disastrous consequences for European, especially Germany's, export.

It now becomes obvious that China could rescue us all

China is still a too a large degree directed economy. But, it is not a communistic one anymore. It follows the same insane principles like the financial capitalism although it sits on more than 2 trillion of US Dollar reserves which will, if the Dollar further declines, which is more than likely, loose it's value.

Other than the free market apologetics of the 'western free democracies' did it until the casino capitalism started it's long and painful decline, China didn't indulge in liberalisations and deregulations. It has always been a free market – domestically.

This has to do with the fact that inside China there are not that many private investors that could seek a lifting of regulations. Foreign investors instead are caught by regulation and control that the West always criticises when it comes to WTO negotiations.

Worldwide, the steel prices are rising as everyone hears about the suddenly increased Chinese demand. In Russia, the steel industry celebrated a 12% growth in July 2009 compared with June 2009, even Japan increased it's steel export by 17%, most of it to China.

But, what does China do with all that steel? Mainstream economists these days explain to us that an economy of more than 1.2 billion people who are trembling with their feet waiting to be allowed to consume since Western life-style has been introduced to China are responsible for the increased demand. That's bullocks. China lives solely on export.

Moreover, to use the imported steel for domestic consumption would be crazy as one would have to change the Dollar reserves for that which would immediately slump the Dollar dramatically – a film the Chinese certainly wouldn't want to watch. No, the truth is that the Chinese state-capitalistic elite had learnt from the West how to build bubbles and to become rich by snowball systems just too well.

The Chinese government, if it was in any way socialistic and cared about their population, could, of course, spend the two trillion US Dollars by investing into infrastructure, social programs, health care and education. By applying some additional Keynesian tools, the Chinese government could create a self-sustaining boom that would, because of the size of the country trigger a world wide recovery.

By investing into alternative energy, China could become the leader of the world without repeating the mistakes of Western industrialisation which so recklessly wasted resources, destroyed natural habitats and exploited human beings.

But, it would mean that China had to be different than other major economies. It would mean to put the priorities right and not have profit maximization rule. And, it would mean to introduce an alternative economic model based on a distribution of wealth – mechanism that solely is defined by productivity increases as well as a social balance neither Capitalism nor Chinese style of 'Communism' is able to provide.

II.

A DEBT-, NOT A CREDIT CRISIS

Debts, not Wage
Increases

President Barack Obama still owes tough decisions concerning the American economic model of the past decades. The consequences will be felt in Europe and throughout the world. With worst economic figures coming to light these days European manufacturers suffer from the American decline heavily.

The more the state's ability to stabilise profit share and demand reached its natural limitation the consumer indebtedness entered centre stage. This kind of privatised Keynesianism totally lay in the neo-liberal trend of privatisations.

Not the state is building up deficits in order to help the economy with creating profitable demand but the vast majority of citizens take out loans and mortgages in order to finance consumption the level of wages would not suggest they could afford.

Commonly, wage-dumping would strangle domestic demand and lead the economy into agony which we have witnessed in Germany over the past ten years. But, in the US wages were brutally brought down in the 1980ies. For 70% of all American employees the real wage in 1989 has been below the level of 1979. For the bottom 40% in those 10 years wages decreased by 10% while the 1990ies only brought stagnation.

In December 2000 the real net wages in the private US economy (except for management positions) has been 5% lower than in 1979.

The reaction has been longer working hours and second and third jobs.

Also after 2000 the median family income did not increase significantly although it was said that there has been an incredible economic boom. Nevertheless, the US reported a steadily growing consumption share of 3% between 1985 and 1995 and by 4.3% thereafter. Rapidly increasing consumption let the US economy but because of huge imports also throughout the world grow at pace rate.

It has not only been the American upper class but also the family of 'Joe the Plumber' did not tighten their belt despite shrinking wages.

The growing disparity between income and spending at first was bridged by knocking the piggy bank and later by taking out loans and mortgages. The indebtedness of American households had reached unbelievable 80% of the available income in the 1980ies, in the year 2000 it was almost 100%. The ultimate kick then came after 2001 when low interest mortgages amid increasing real estate prices created the perfect environment for average households to accept ridiculous loan proposals.

This helped the US economy get out of the recession after the dotcom – bubble of the Clinton-Gore administration burst. The bulk of the mortgages hasn't been used for building or buying houses but financing consumption. That's how an artificial building boom became the lifeline of an otherwise ailing economic system.

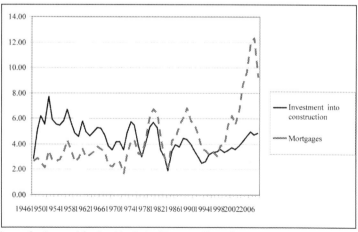

Source for data used for Graphic: Federal Reserve 'Flow of Funds'

The real estate – hype resulted in an over-indebtedness of the American consumers by 125% of the disposable income at the end of 2006.

These loans were not used for luxury goods but increasingly often for financing relatively banal issues such as paying school fees or hospital bills. Because of the shrinking wages the standard of living of middle class families could only be maintained by furnishing mortgage loans to bolster their spending power.

The Consumption Expenditure Survey (CEX) which doesn't include the richest parts of society shows that the share of luxury clothes, jewellery, travel, fun parks, entertainment electronics and holiday homes in relation to the disposable income since the 1980ies is constantly declining.

On the other hand, the CEX share of education and health care has drastically increased mostly because of the inflation in those fields of public subsistence where the state has pulled out.

In other words: in order to bring America back on track, the new administration will have to make sure that life becomes affordable again for the ordinary citizens. Privatised Keynesianism doesn't work. Private healthcare and education lead to inflation and become unaffordable for those who really need it while they appear to be advantageous for those who are better off.

Mr. Obama has a lot of work to do and he can't do it the Clinton-way as there is no room for manoeuvring unless he creates bubbles as well. But, the American middle class has already eaten up their savings and houses a long time ago.

APPROACHING THE FINAL LEG

Obligations are still out there - next crash will be with depositor's money

The take over of investment banks like Merrill Lynch and Lehman Brothers by commercial banks such as Bank of America and Barclays in the days after 14th September 2008, the "Black Sunday" culminated in the transformation of the last major investment banks, Goldman Sachs and Morgan Stanley, into commercial banks.

This desperate move will limit these institutions' ability to create further bubbles as commercial banks are much stricter regulated and need to show deposits to back their lending exposure.

On the positive side one can see why on Sunday, 21st September 2008 Goldman Sachs and Morgan Stanley were able to take deposits giving them a major resource base while they will also have the same access as other commercial banks to emergency loan programs.

"The Federal Reserve will also lend directly to Goldman, Morgan and Merrill's London-based broker dealer subsidiaries" the Financial Times reported on 22nd September 2008.

Stock markets worldwide from Asian markets to German DAX celebrated the decisions with a firework of skyrocketing indices. In the U.S. equity markets rose sharply after the bail-out and nationalisation of Fannie and Freddie, although the outstanding liabilities of some 5,400 billion US Dollars are still there.

Once the damage had been done the European governments are quick to blame the U.S. but this is also due to the fact that one doesn't want to help the U.S. bail out their investment banks. The U.S. government's nationalisation policy towards Fannie Mae and Freddie Mac sends out the wrong signal. The problem can't be fixed within the system. One would have to rather think outside the box.

Nevertheless, the Financial Times headlined on 8th September 2008 "Risk appetite returns after US rescue" reporting that Nasdaq jumped 1.4%, Dow Jones 2.4%, the S&P 500 financials sector adding 5.2% in short order. Only one day later this was all hot air again.

The frequency of the bounces is increasing every day now.

COMMERCIAL BANKS BECAME LAST RESORT

The fact that after the rescue mission of the FED lending started again should cause worries. The take-overs of investment banks by commercial banks is a logic step as these were the only ones which still could do it, because these banks hold deposits.

Frightening to know that the craziness will continue and go into the last round: taking deposits, real money from real people, and gamble with those funds. Because the debt obligations and liabilities are still out there, the next crash will not be like the previous ones of 11th August 2007 and 14th September 2008 which happened in the virtual reality world of Wall Street's casino but will destroy real wealth, real industries and real purchasing power.

The capital and debt concentration will culminate in the replacement of the profit-oriented creative destruction by the destruction of creativity, productivity and wealth.

The collapse of the financial system is not a random development. It is rather the logic of a system creating financial bubbles standing in no relation with production, aren't in line with productivity and growth other than having a grip on the wealth produced by others.

THE OWNERS OF THE FEDERAL RESERVE

As there is, according to the UK's House Banking Committee Staff report of 1976, a linear connection between N.M. Rothschild, the Bank of England which ultimately control the Federal Reserve Banks through their stockholdings of bank stock and their subsidiary firms in New York, it is clear that the FED is not left with any choice but to bail out investment banks however naughty their behaviour has been.

The two principal Rothschild representatives in New York, J. P. Morgan Co. and Kuhn, Loeb & Co. were the firms which set up the Jekyll Island Conference at which the Federal Reserve Act was drafted, who directed the subsequent successful campaign to have the plan enacted into law by Congress, and who purchased the controlling amounts of stock in the Federal Reserve Bank of New York in 1914. These firms had their principal officers appointed to the Federal Reserve Board of Governors. In 1914 a few families (blood or business related) owning controlling stock in existing banks such as in New York City caused those banks to purchase controlling shares in the Federal Reserve regional banks. Examination of the charts and the text in the House Banking Committee Staff Report of August 1976 and the current stockholders list of the 12 regional Federal Reserve Banks show this same family control.

THE FED IS LESS AMERICAN THAN MOST PEOPLE MAY THINK IT IS

The line goes from Nathan Meyer Rothschild, London and the Bank of England, London to Morgan Grenfell, Morgan & Cie, Paris, Lazard Freres, Paris, J.P. Morgan Co. New York, J. Henry Schroder Banking Corp., Schroder Bank, Hamburg & Berlin, Lehman Brothers, New York, Elsie & William Rockefeller, New York, Isabel & Percy Rockefeller, New York, James Paul Warburg, New York to Sir Gordon Richardson, Governor of the Bank of England in 1973 who at the same time has been board member of J. Henry Schroder, New York as well as Lloyds Bank, and to the Belgian Relief Commission under Emile Francoui. This extract of the charts of who owns the Federal Reserve may illustrate how international the financial market actually is.

It is not only the "Anglo-Saxon" model of investment banks that collapsed, it is also German, Belgian, French and others. It is clear that the owners of the FED will fight for rescuing their stakes by whatever means, by taking each other over, printing additional money, taking new deposits and lending to each other to win time. But, the financial market can't be fixed that way, but maybe it's final collapse postponed a bit, let's say over election days in the U.S., Great-Britain and Germany as during a depression voters might not trust existing political structures anymore.

What started with Bear Stearns in March 2008 has now come to an end. Wall Street is not the same anymore. A 75 years long era came to an end, not a happy one, though. The owners of the Federal Reserve are bailing themselves out.

CONSPIRACY AGAINST THE TAXPAYER

Reporting from London, 3rd April 2009

The terminology is misleading. Instead of calling it a 'credit crisis' we should rather speak about a 'debt crisis'. As money doesn't simply vanish one may ask who holds all these debts and obligations. 'Debit' on one side of the balance sheet means 'Credit' on the other. But, what should one expect in respect of accuracy when dealing with an industry that loves to use misleading terms such as "profit warning" when in fact losses are made, "negative growth" when the economy is shrinking or "slowdown" to describe a fierce recession?!

If anything has become clear at the G20 summit in London, it was that the continental European and the American – British camps have parted company. French President Nicolas Sarkozy and German Chancellor Angela Merkel had vowed to crack down on the Anglo-Saxon/American business model.

When asked by me whether she was satisfied by the compromise negotiated at the G20 summit that was to impose regulation on hedge funds which British analysts feared could shut down *The City*, Mrs. Merkel smiled and pointed out that like in any other industry the product would have to pass muster. She added that "there won't be a world without financial markets" but that one would have to make sure that "the risks are limited".

Nothing too worrying for hedge funds managers and investment bankers, though, who are only told to behave and not indulge in a way of the previous excesses they have had. Instead, new opportunities for debt-bubble – building are given by US President Barack Obama and British Prime Minister Gordon Brown by printing money for what they call stimulus packages.

OFFSHORE TAX HAVENS TO ADHERE TO OECD STANDARDS – IN THEORY

Another important point in the G20 talks have been off-shore tax havens which were said to come under similar scrutiny. It is also clear that nobody will in all earnest police these black holes of the financial markets in which an estimated quarter of the world's GDP is laundered as an investment banker speaking on condition of anonymity told me.

Shutting down tax havens would be a good idea but in reality the G20 only decided to impose new standards which will be interesting to watch whether these will really be adhered to or whether bankers will, with a twinkle in their eyes, say that yes they apply new regulations while in fact nobody can control it. This kind of self-regulation is like allowing monkeys mind a banana plant.

Left alone the manager remunerations and bonus schemes will be slightly different. But, while the focus is directed on certainly outrageous bonus payments such as the 165 million Dollars for AIG managers, the 93.2 *billion* Dollars which the taxpayer seems to be happy to transfer to the shareholders of AIG's clients Goldman Sachs and Deutsche Bank AG are barely debated as the Financial Times noted. Manager-bashing is chic these days but only distracts from the real issue.

STIMULUS PACKAGES – LET OTHERS PAY THE BILL FOR THE PARTY

Other misconceptions are widespread these days, too. The so called 'stimulus packages' President Obama and Prime Minister Brown are continuously bringing forward are not directed at any producing industries (which hardly exist in their countries anyway) but will feed the debt bubble before a tiny bit may trickle down from the hedge funds and investment banks to the real economy and consumer.

Seen from the American point of view President Obama is right to print money even though this will cause inflation. But, so far the upper class in the US doesn't fear inflation as a threat to their assets and they are right not to – as long as there is no global inflation and as long as US treasury bonds are still bought. Germany and much of the Euro-zone are facing years of deflation and China has no choice but to hold on to its two trillion US Dollar reserves as it doesn't want to see those become completely worthless. On the other hand, and that's the only reason why the American upper-class is supporting President Obama, by inflating its currency the US more or less elegantly gets rid off its debts.

Only if EU and others decide to give up on the US as a market, then of course the Dollar would slip and inflation become a problem for the upper class in the US.

CONTINENTAL EU & US/UK IN SAME BOAT, NOT SAME LIFE-RAFT, THOUGH

Continental Europe, being led by France and Germany, takes a different stance. The European Central Bank (ECB) which had been modelled on the German Bundesbank is eager to fight inflation as only this is seen as a threat to Europe's upper class assets. That's why ECB President Jean-Claude Trichet reluctantly lowered the base rate by another 0.25% while the US and Great-Britain expected a clearer signal to come out of Frankfurt.

Germany's calculation could be that while everybody else is up for stimulus packages (which eventually help the German export-leaning industry) accumulating huge debts, Germany will stand strong and tall, rather attracting foreign investment than scaring markets by running into over-indebtedness.

It is true: all those stimulus packages only feed the debt bubble which again will provide for the playground of hedge funds and investment banks. The recovery of the latter doesn't mark the end of the recession at all but merely the manifestation of the dreadful income and wealth distribution of the past that led to the present crisis once more by taking from the poor and giving to the rich.

Again, the citizens are asked to pay for those debts. According to the BBC the British taxpayer will have to come up with some additional 1,250 pounds per year for a generation while many analysts think that the figure was too low. It would be rather modest, indeed, as the US taxpayer so far is confronted with a bill of 17,000 Dollars per year for all the packages and bailouts Bush and Obama initiated. So far all these are debts and one may wonder if they were ever to be paid. A good deal of it will be paid anyhow by developing countries which had starved out of their population huge Dollar reserves. Further inflation of the Dollar will impose the US' debt onto the poor countries holding treasury bonds and Dollar reserves.

INSTEAD OF HANDING LIFE-LINE TO OWNERS ONE FINANCE PRODUCTION

It would make more sense for the British government to guarantee new debts for businesses rather than guaranteeing old debts. Likewise, the US government would create a *real* stimulus of some 200 billion US Dollars for the wider public by bringing mortgage interest rates down to 4.5% rather than pouring money into dead banks. Losers would be major shareholders such as institutional investors or ultra rich individuals. On the other hand these have been pampered over the last 2 decades by tax-legislation as well as de-regulations, lucrative privatisations and liberalisations.

Germany, especially, had been generous in granting tax relief for major corporations and rich private owners during the red-green coalition government of Chancellor Gerhard Schröder who also rolled out the red carpet for hedge funds and private equity firms. By this policy Germany invited those parts of the Anglo-Saxon/American business model in that it now unilaterally blames for all the evil. But, it is not fair to hold these firms and their managers responsible without mentioning the beneficiaries of the insane profit maximisation.

The Financial Times Deutschland (FTD) reported just days before the London Summit that the DAX listed major corporations in 2009 are to pay out 22.5 billion Euros in dividends to their shareholders. The average dividend return on investment at the 30 DAX listed corporations has risen to 4.4% (more than in the years between 2000 and 2005) in this year in which analysts engage in 'doom and gloom' talk.

RE-DISTRIBUTION OF WEALTH FROM BOTTOM TO TOP BIGGEST PROBLEM

The German unions Ver.di sensed that something went wrong and cited that "by denying sufficient wage increases in the past 10 years employees had been deprived of 500 billion Euros while the tax policy has additionally enhanced the re-distribution of wealth from bottom to top by another 500 billion Euros. By this, German corporations and owners have gained a trillion Euros in the last 10 years in additional profits."

Meanwhile, the OECD said at the eve of the London Summit that it expected the crisis in the OECD countries to take a toll of 25 million jobs and by this double the unemployment ratio of 5.7% (in 2007) while the real economy in the OECD countries is expected to shrink by 4.2%.

According to Eurostat, the industrial production in the Euro-zone has dropped between January 2008 and January 2009 by 34.2%. This can hardly be called 'recession', it is depression.

German exports, the backbone of any *Aufschwung* (up-swing) of recent years collapsed in January of 2009 by 20% indicating that the annual 100 billion Euros of surplus (in 2007 it had been 170 billion Euros) are far from being rescued by the 'stimulus packages' of Chancellor Merkel's government. Ironically, one could say that President Obama is of better help.

SO WHAT SHOULD BE DONE IN ORDER TO GET OUT OF THE MESS?

A clean cut would be the only way out. One should nullify all debts and declare financial excesses illegal while wealth needs to be re-distributed from the top to the middle class and bottom of society. A fair balance has to be sought and maintained.

This is the key to solving the crisis. We are not in a credit crisis but in a debt crisis.

Debts on one side of the balance sheet mean that there are credits on the other side.

And, as money doesn't simply vanish, but only changes ownership we should have a close look whereto the money is gone and at who holds all these obligations.

The danger if we do not do exactly that will be to prolong the decline during which our democracies may slip into dictatorships, fascism and major wars.

The liquidity bomb made from debts that is hanging over us will cause a financial tsunami once it drops.

The citizens are right to expect the state to influence the economic course. But, the question is not *whether* the state becomes a stakeholder in the economy but in whose interest, with which goals and at what cost. The main question here will be who is going to pay.

The present crisis is a crisis of an economic system which only produces for profit and not for actual demand. Major corporations which even during an economic up-swing engage in wage dumping, downsizing and axing investments and research capacities in order to increase the shareholder value minimize economic growth and distributable wealth.

A financial system that dumps billions in snowball systems instead of investing such in real production doesn't live up to the tasks of the economy and waived its right to exist. Today's economic system is not only socially unjust and environmentally dreadful. It is simply anti-economic as it destroys production. Particularly SMEs are continuously disadvantaged by the extreme income concentration at the upper class.

Said income distribution inflates the financial bubbles while strangling demand on the goods markets. This leads to a systematic misdirection of the real economy, resulting in the creation of massive overcapacities on the one side and a dramatic under-supply on the other.

It has been the neo-liberal policy of EU Commission and member state governments that laid the seed for the present catastrophe by every single deregulation, liberalisation and privatisation of public subsistence. Currently, those advocates of neo-liberalism try to save this economic model by injecting taxpayer's money and by socializing the losses of the shareholders and owners.

The vast majority of the citizens shall now pay the bill of the party they have not even been invited to only in order to allow the upper class to have another party from which again employees, SMEs, unemployed, pensioners and every kid in a public school once more shall be excluded.[4]

---

4   Handelsblatt 21st November 2008
     FTD 24th March 2009
     FTD 30th March 2009
     FTD 31st March 2009
     EUROSTAT releases 33,34,35,37,38,39/20

HAVE THEY HEARD THE SHOT THAT HAS BEEN FIRED?

Strasbourg 5ᵗʰ May 2009

EU Commissioners Spidla & Huebner: "road to recovery"

The differences couldn't be bigger: while Euro-Group president, Luxembourg's Prime Minister Jean-Claude Juncker, warns of possible social unrest and dangers of up-risings in lieu of the dramatic economic decline, EU Commissioners Danuta Huebner and Vladimir Spidla, responsible for social affairs and labour market in the EU, praise the "cohesion policy" and the introduction of the hire & fire principle known as 'flexicurity' under the so called 'Lisbon strategy' as the "road to recovery".

Under the so called "cohesion policy" social partners were locked into round table talks between employers and unions and forced to agree to social cuts and flexible labour conditions which many NGOs and leftists branded as EU-wide wage- and standard dumping.

Ahead of this week's 'Employment Summit', EU Commission president Jose Manuel Barroso emphasised in the plenary of the European Parliament that "the Employment summit gives an opportunity to keep employment at the top of the EU agenda where it belongs."

"I want this Summit to yield concrete, tangible results. I am hopeful that it will", Mr Barroso said adding that it was "another milestone in an ongoing process that started well before the crisis – a process of co-operation between the Commission, the Member States and the social partners - which will go on throughout the crisis and beyond."

He finally concluded that "we cannot separate our economic and our social agenda: There can be no economic recovery on the foundations of social collapse, just as there can be no social progress in an economic desert."

Such an almost apologetic belief in the collapsing economic system can be witnessed elsewhere, too.

THEY DID IT AGAIN!

In line with the Anglo-American dictum according to which thoughts are stronger than reality FED chairman Ben Bernanke announced that across the Atlantic things seem to be less dim as expected, agencies like Bloomberg are eager to report.

The reality check condoned by the International Monetary Fund (IMF) revealed that the global financial system will lose some 4.1 trillion US Dollars between 2007 and 2010, double of what had been estimated so far.

Nevertheless, US President Barack Obama's rhetoric induced glimmers of hope as the first quarter of 2009 results of several financial institutions that months ago had been considered clinically dead were extremely positive.

JP Morgan reported profit of 2.1 billion Dollars, Wells Fargo 3 billion, Goldman Sachs 1.8 billion, Citigroup 1.2 billion and Bank of America 4.2 billion. Suddenly, all seemed to be like in the good old days as speculative money returned to Wall Street. Within 6 weeks Dow Jones gained by 25%, stocks of banks like Citigroup skyrocketed by some 400%.

The real economy, however, doesn't benefit again, also like in the days of the Casino Capitalism. Moreover, the New York Times revealed that the Obama-administration allowed the banks to employ creative accountancy tricks and also the Fortune magazine admitted that the "usual accountancy standards did no longer apply". US finance minister Timothy Geithner, familiar with bubble-building since the Clinton-administration, makes it possible for banks to transform otherwise un-sellable financial trash into credit-positions on their balance sheets:

The Obama-administration allows financial institutions to "re-assess" the toxic assets, commercial debt obligations (CDOs) and mortgage backed securities (MBS) as well as asset backed securities (ABS) which in reality were heavily over-valued. Bankers now may legally assume an unrealistic high value for such papers on the balance sheet.

A second trick is also allowed: institutions may negate their debt to a large degree and thirdly, the Obama-administration provides for generous write-off possibilities that shall minimize the institutions losses – at least on paper.

All the above allows banks like Citigroup which had accumulated 2.5 billion Dollars in losses celebrate a 1.2 billion profit and were starting to pay out bonuses again. Like ordinary criminals these people return to the scene of their crime but obviously not with a bad conscience at all. They did it again and will do it again and again unless one stops them.

EURO-GROUP PRESIDENT JUNCKER: "SOCIAL UNREST LIKELY"

The president of the Euro-Group, those member states who adopted the Euro, Jean-Claude Juncker, prime minister of Luxembourg, warned of "social unrest" and by this showed that at least he had all his senses together. He certainly is aware of what is going to happen.

Hans-Olaf Henkel, former president of Germany's federation of industrialists, *Bund Deutscher Industrie (BDI)*, and a outspoken neo-liberal hardliner, told me end of April in Paris that he felt like the "system's lone defender". To my question whether, if the present economic system proves so obviously to be anti-economical by producing only for profit and not for actual demand leading to overcapacities and un-sustainability it was not the time to question the economic model he replied that there was "no alternative".

"There is no compromise possible. Some people seem to think that we can fix it by meddling with principles and be a bit more social or a bit more liberal. The truth is that it is rather digital: zero or one, black or white."

Here, Mr Henkel is certainly right. Many commentators who are not economists indulge in the dream of the crisis opening a door for the *Third Way* but how could that been achieved given the fact that the neo-classical model is not based on economic theory but only on ideology? And, how could the 'survival of the fittest credo' of such ideology ever be reconciled with an economic system serving the people using economic capacities and rising productivity for social protection and not for profit maximisation?

III.

THE ANGLO-AMERICAN VIRTUAL REALITY CASINO

Bonuses are Back!

The biggest 'losers' of the crisis, Citigroup, Goldman Sachs, Morgan Stanley and JP Morgan Chase who all received billions from *Uncle Sam* paid huge bonuses to their top management. Citigroup had received 45 billion Dollars in state aid (which resulted in the US government becoming the biggest shareholder of the bank holding 34%) but this didn't hold the board of the bank back from paying 5.3 billion Dollars in bonuses. On top of that, the bank had announced a record loss of 27.7 billion Dollars for 2008. Nevertheless, 738 Citigroup bankers thought their big success had to be rewarded and took more than a million Dollars each. Maybe it was also the thought that they might soon loose their jobs that let them steal taxpayer's money. One would never know when it was the last time, they may have thought. But also JP Morgan Chase and Morgan Stanley paid higher bonuses than there was profit.

In total the US' biggest 9 banks had received 175 billion Dollars in aid thanking this generous rescue mission of the Obama administration by paying out bonuses of 32.6 billion.[5]

What may appear as a scandal, and sure it is, is also designed to distract our focus. By putting the outrage about the impertinent bonuses for unsuccessful managers into the centre of the debate it is diverting the limelight from the real beneficiaries of the system, UHNWIs, Ultra High Net Worth Individuals (as Merrill Lynch refers to rich shareholders and owners) to their helpers and partners in crime,

---

5   Spiegel online 31st July 2009

the hedge funds, private equity firms, their top managers, brokers and investment bankers.

What is also more important for the real economy than the bonuses of some ruthless managers is the fact that the banks are still not willing to supply SMEs with funds. The European Central Bank (ECB) announced[6] that the supply with money dramatically shrank by 35 billion Euros in June 2009. This really affects the economy and is even more scandalous than the entire bonus schemes. How can it be that banks are receiving rescue packages from the taxpayer and not fulfil their obligation in the financial system but rather pay their shareholders and managers?

That's why the state's parachutes should immediately be transformed into public ownership rights. The argument that publicly owned banks had also produced losses and were not managed better than the private banks can be countered by pointing out that the public banks had participated in the transactions far away from the core business and that such risky business should simply not be allowed or be banned to casinos. On the other hand, a publicly owned bank could be forced to hand out loans badly needed for the real economy. Anything else the bank's management engaged in could be declared illegal. That's how simple it could be, but instead the governments seem to be in bed with the shareholders who take advantage of the rescue missions by politicians from both sides of the Atlantic.

The recovery of stock market during the summer of 2009 only is proof for the next insanity that any government involvement be it by creating 'bad banks' or by bailing out or by underwriting banks provoke: the absurd trickling down of funds to institutional investors who start building new bubbles again. In other words, all these beautiful rescue missions our political leaders who until recently told us about the necessity to tighten our belts and adhere to fiscal austerity because the pockets of the state were empty, are pulling out of the drawers have only one effect: to feed a Hausse that will finance the next Ponzi-scheme, snowball system or health care, education and alternative energy bubble, thus making once more those richer who by their miss-speculations had gotten us into the trouble. No SME,

---

6   Spiegel online 27th July 2009

inventor, carpenter, manufacturer, plumber or local shop owner will be rescued but instead will be confronted with higher indirect taxes which are the result of the failure of our political leaders to talk straight and get tough rather than handing out yet another lifeline to the financial junkies who laugh about the stupidity of the public that even creates so called Bad Banks recently. One can summarise it by saying that it is designed to socialise the bank's losses. But, potential future profits are not entirely out of reach for the taxpayer also and that may be seen as the main reason why only a few banks so far took advantage of the government's offers. In Germany, WestLB and hypo Real Estate (HRE) who in the near future won't be profitable have made use of the band bank facility. But, banks such as Deutsche Bank AG or Commerzbank AG who both are making huge profits again, may as well keep his toxic papers on the books for yet another while. One advantage is, of course, that one doesn't necessarily have to see the real value of said toxic papers as they can still be hidden in the balance sheets. Once a bank had dumped those in the bad bank, nothing had been won by the bank as the real losses become visible. As the bank still would be liable for such losses resulting from it's toxic papers this would diminish it's prospects on the stock markets. It would also lay bare the risk exposure and in a way, let's say it, the stupidity of it's management. No bank wishes to be seen in that light. In other words: only a bank which otherwise faces bankruptcy will be interested in availing of bad bank facility.

On top of that, the rating agencies have yet not decided whether to gout the bad bank construct or not. But, the fundamental question whether the banks may treat the state guaranteed credit line as state bonds or whether they would still be required to hold the equivalent as capital on stock. This problem illustrates once more how bizarre it is to make legal requirements dependent on the mood of rating agencies such as Moody's, Fitch's and Standard & Poor. More significant, in fact, may be at the moment that the suffering in the bank's board rooms has not been great enough, yet. At the moment the market value of many of those toxic assets are pointing upwards which does not mean that these obligations aren't as toxic as they were thought to be. Whoever has a closer look at the US' statistics knows about the over-indebtedness of American households that has compensated shrinking wages over much more than a decade by ever higher consumer credits and mortgages. As a result debts have been piled up which can never be paid back, even if prosperous times came back in a few years. There is also no reason to believe in that fairy tale that companies whose capital stock had been to tiny for surviving in economic more stabile times and that have been forced into over-indebtedness by Private Equity sharks will survive the current crisis. To think that commercial debt obligations (CDO's) and other papers that bundled such bad credits are yet to make headwind is a result of the institutionalised insanity of the financial markets. On those speculative markets not a fundamental value is traded but anything that looks promising to be sold for more than it has been bought for. This expectation is well and alive at present because the US government prints enormous amounts of cash in order to reanimate the market for structured credit obligations. Since a couple of months a program of the American Central Bank, the Federal Reserve, buys up and by this takes off the market mortgage backed securities and commercial obligations totalling 750 billion US Dollars, most of which are stemming from troubled Freddy Mac and Fannie Mae. On top of that, US treasury secretary Timothy Geithner tries to motivate vulture funds and private equity firms by state-backed guarantees to buy the toxic trash off the banks. By this method, the banks shall get rid off toxic assets of up to one trillion US Dollars. These are not the papers held by Fannie & Freddie but the real Sub-prime mortgage trash. This program de-facto can be seen as a state-run 'Bad Bank' and has created in October alone an additional demand of some 40 billion US Dollars which may not sound too much in relation to the market volume of several thousand billions but on a speculative market the mere indication that a certain product sees an increase in demand is usually enough encouragement to other speculators to jump onto the band wagon.

This way once more a self enhancing effect creates artificial demand and let's prices go up. There are many examples for such absurd theatre: When, for instance, more than 40 years ago US President Richard Nixon launches his appeasement policy towards China, some financial junkies in London started an intensive trade with ancient Chinese state obligations from Emperor's times and although none of these papers had ever made a single cent in profit for decades the prices paid for that trash skyrocketed.

Of course, nobody expected at that time that the People's Republic of China would ever resume interest payment on these antiques. But, everybody in the market calculated with an increased demand because of the nearing of the US and China and solely because of such sentiment the prices increased. Those who managed to get out of the market in time made a fortune on these worthless and useless obligations. It will be similar with the present hype about the worthless toxic papers or those bank stocks which have created a sheer rally of a thousand per cent in the past 6 months although none of the problems that have caused the financial crash had been solved.

Not even half of the toxic depots have been written off so far, and the world economic crisis continues at pace rate. But, the financial- and stock markets are blooming again. Is it Goldman Sachs, JP Morgan or Deutsche Bank AG, one stands tall again. And, while most of the engineering and manufacturing companies in Manchester or Stuttgart have to worry about their re-financing as credit lines are cut, private equity sharks can bath in cheap money keeping them afloat.

If the goal had been to re-install a system of ever lasting growth and speculation in the virtual reality casino, than the 'bad banks' and the bailing out of banks as well as the supply with cheap money has been the right order of battle.

Of course, the bank's new profits are of same quality as have been those before the crash. Virtual reality gains resulting from a gigantic snowball system in which more or less dubious commercial papers are sold at ever higher prices that are pushed up by exceeding credit lines - until the next crash comes. It is only logic that bankers and investment fund managers aren't too much concerned about the next crash as their task is to produce short term results for the next quarter of a year. The short term success is the goal. And, another reason why bankers and fund managers look into the future rather relaxed can be found in the reassurance by the state that they won't be let down. 'Too big to fail' has been the credo in even relatively small cases such as the German SME - bank 'IKB' or the completely useless Hypo Real Estate (HRE) in which the German government buried totally unnecessarily 160 billion Euros that swiftly ended up in the pockets of rich Deutsche Bank AG shareholders. In light of this it becomes understandable that German banks are not very interested in the "bad bank" or the 480 billion Euros worth of state guarantees by the German government body "Soffin" from which only less than half were drawn so far. Commerzbank AG for instance just returned two thirds of the state guarantees as these cost money, just like when making use of the "bad bank". The de facto reassurance by the state, instead, doesn't cost a single cent.

In a way, the vulture funds doped by the US taxpayer's funds function like a "bad bank" as they take on all the financial trash that currently floats around. In fact, the rescue mission by the US government in hopeless cases such as the insurance conglomerate AIG which had re-insured toxic assets worth 441 billion Dollars, or the equally questionable rescuing of mortgage giants Fannie Mae and Freddie Mac has swept billions of taxpayer's money into the pockets of the hot society of the financial world. In case of AIG it has been 93.2 billion US Dollars of which 11.9 billion Dollars were paid to Deutsche Bank AG, almost as much as Investment Bank Goldman Sachs which received 12.9 billion Dollars in compensation for failed credit derivatives. If the state had not jumped in, the banks had to write it off. Instead, they are paying dividends to shareholders and bonuses to their fund managers and investment bankers.

But, not only in the US and Germany are there generous state-organized money spinners. Seen from banker's- and shareholder's point of view an incredibly lucrative "Bad Bank" – model has been implemented in Ireland. NAMA, a state body designed to buy up all problematic loans and mortgages, will pay more than 77 billion Euros for loans of which more than 50% are not serviced anymore. Nevertheless, the Irish state will give the banks state obligations in exchange for that at face value without any deductions. The Irish taxpayer will have to pay these state obligations and it's interest day by day until the state is bankrupt. Before that, of course, any social spending and public investment will be cut back to the bare minimum. The stock markets reacted enthusiastically and the stocks of the two major banks on Emerald Island, Allied Irish Bank and Bank of Ireland, skyrocketed by 30%. On the other side financial institutions and banks are still on strike when it comes to supplying the economy with badly needed liquidity. This is the main tool in the fight between banks and the state and it is not since yesterday that major banks are not fulfilling their obligations in advancing loans and credit lines to industry and

SMEs but since a couple of years. Especially since it has become more lucrative to gamble in the casinos of NASDAQ, DAX and 'The City' in London than following the core business of traditional banking, all major institutions have become investment banks who wish to see their commercial risk being covered by the state and their losses be taken over by the taxpayer. An alternative scenario would, indeed, be possible. The state could, for instance, force the banks to increase their capital stock. Those banks which are unable to do so, should be forced to place their toxic assets in a "Bad Bank" without compensation and write it off. Instead of guaranteeing the toxic papers the state could then go and supply the 'good banks' which by then might have burnt all their cash, with fresh funds and combine this with the obligation for the banks to issue credit lines and loans to industries, SMEs and private households. The advantage of this scenario for the taxpayer would be that he is not only left with the trash but also has a grip on the profitable active positions of the banks balance sheets. By this method, public interest and the taxpayer are protected as every Euro or Dollar being invested into those banks will result in ownership rights any other investor would always seek in a free market economy. The dreadful privatisation of profits and simultaneous socialisation of the losses would once and for all be brought to an end. A good one for state and taxpayer. Sweden has exercised exactly that after it's banking crisis in 1994. Nordbanken and Götabanken had been nationalised without compensation for the shareholders and the taxpayer owned not only a dump full of trash paper, but also the good part of these banks which indeed did produce some revenue. Unfortunately, after successful reanimation of the banks these have been returned into private ownership again. It took only a short while until the private owners and their bankers started the same insanity all over again. It has to be clear that public ownership without accompanying regulations that eliminate such speculative transactions that had led to the previous disaster wouldn't make sense. On the other hand, if such financial craziness was banned, would there be such an interest in private ownership of banks? Probably much less. So far there has been no progress in terms of better regulation that would protect us in the future.

Ralph T. Niemeyer

DON'T THROW THE LIQUIDITY – BOMB!

March 2009

At a time when the British economy which over 16 years has been the fastest growing economy in Europe is plummeting because of toxic assets amounting to a multiple of the UK's annual GDP, one may ask whether one should rather bail out the citizens than asking same to continue to spend taxpayer's money for bailing out banks and their shareholders.

The BBC had reported at the end of February that the taxpayers have so far covered some 1.3 trillion pounds (the entire UK's annual GNP) in bailing out banks. Germany and France, it was said had no hedge funds industry and therefore were not as badly hit as *The City* which accounts for some 67% of Great-Britain's GDP.

The truth, however, is that some 1,400 hedge funds, most of them registered in the UK which is famous for it's liberal banking law, were operating across Europe. At that time German Chancellor Gerhard Schröder had rolled out the red carpet for hedge funds and private equity firms that brought down the real economy.

Nevertheless, Germany will probably be the last country which will still be given credit, even long time after the UK and others have filed for bankruptcy. It is also, because Germany only joined the financially insane Anglo-Saxon business model that late that not much harm could be done.

MONEY DOESN'T SIMPLY VANISH, IT ONLY CHANGES OWNERSHIP

So far, no honest and workable scenario has been presented by anyone.

All EU governments and foremost the EU Commission seem to be reluctant to apply the necessary radical changes that would not prolong the decline but rather get the real economy back on track. Remember, it was the producing industries which were doing well before the hedge fund – junkies and private equity pirates bought, stripped, scrapped, sold them.

Instead of bailing out the scam artists who got us into the trouble one should rather secure jobs, production lines and SMEs.

Our economies' elite which benefited shamelessly by deregulated markets nowadays calls for the state as flooding the real economy by public funds alone can not protect their property and income. But there are hundreds of millions of people in the EU who fear for their jobs, savings and social existence.

These citizens are right to expect the state to influence the economic course. But, the question is not *whether* the state becomes a stakeholder in the economy but in whose interest, with which goals and at what cost. The main question here will be who is going to pay.

The present crisis is a crisis of an economic system which only produces for profit and not for actual demand. Major corporations which even during an economic up-swing engage in wage dumping, downsizing and axing investments and research capacities in order to increase the shareholder value minimize economic growth and distributable wealth.

SMEs CONTINUOUSLY DISADVANTAGED

A financial system that dumps billions in snowball systems instead of investing such in real production doesn't live up to the tasks of the economy and waived its right to exist. Today's economic system is not only socially unjust and environmentally dreadful. It is simply anti-economic as it destroys production. Particularly SMEs are continuously disadvantaged by the extreme income concentration at the upper class.

Said income distribution inflates the financial bubbles while strangling demand on the goods markets. This leads to a systematic misdirection of the real economy, resulting in the creation of massive overcapacities on the one side and a dramatic under-supply on the other.

This inevitably becomes a global threat for production and productivity, jobs and wealth, innovation and creativity.

It has been the neo-liberal policy of EU Commission and member state governments that laid the seed for the present catastrophe by every single deregulation, liberalisation and privatisation of public subsistence. Currently, those advocates of neo-liberalism try to save this economic model by injecting taxpayer's money and by socializing their losses.

The vast majority of the citizens shall now pay the bill of the party they have not even been invited to only in order to allow the upper class to have another party of which again employees, SMEs, unemployed, pensioners and every kid in a public school once more shall be excluded.

A REAL ANTI-CRISIS PROGRAM:

Time is ripe for real alternatives. If one really wanted to solve the crisis without laying seeds for the next one, one has to question the legitimacy of the present economic model.

An Anti-Crisis program which stops the economic decline, saves jobs while it prevents the general public from suffering for decades from the trillion-fold fallout of the bursting bubbles is indeed possible and feasible but it requires a completely new economic model in which all can benefit from rises in productivity and accumulated wealth.

Private banks which are responsible for the bubble building and loss of trillions should be nationalised without compensations being paid to its shareholders. Savings accounts should be guaranteed other obligations of said banks only be considered if the real economy or the public be seriously affected.

Strict regulation should ensure the banking sector to fulfil its obligation again by the supply of finance for economically viable businesses and investments, research as well as SMEs and a free current account for everybody. The so called 'investment banking' is to be abolished completely, the trading of derivatives or any form of speculation be prohibited and any dealings with corporations or individuals registered in tax havens and off shore black-holes be made punishable.

Private pension funds which contributed to inflating the bubbles significantly should be nationalised and strictly used for providing pensions for the elderly to ensure they can live in dignity.

Speculative investment vehicles such as hedge funds and private equity firms should be closed down for good.

STATE AID OUGHT TO LEAD TO OWNERSHIP-RIGHTS

State aid for enterprises are certainly the right tool for securing jobs, but said aid should euro by euro result in ownership rights for the public. This should be used to change the way companies are run, not by fixation for increasing the shareholder value but a long-term sustainability. Any kind of stock-option for wage increase - swaps should be prohibited.

The policy of de-nationalisation, liberalisation and unconditional surrender to market dominance has to be made undone. Human basic subsistence such as housing, education and healthcare has to be provided to any person regardless of the personal income situation. Same applies for the access to water, energy, transport and communication services.

Above basic subsistence can be provided in high quality and sufficient quantity only by public, non-profit orientated enterprises.

The neo-liberal privatisation and cut-down policy of the most recent years has led to massive under-supply in many areas.

LET'S BECOME COUNTER-CYCLICAL AND INVEST RIGHT NOW!

It is time to overcome the public investment paralysis. There is enough work around. It simply has to be paid for. Since productivity constantly rises theoretically there shouldn't be a problem to finance public investments but in recent years only shareholders benefited from the increasing productivity.

It is a shame that in rich EU countries like Germany roads, schools and hospitals deteriorate while communal libraries, theatres and leisure centres are under-funded and closed. In order to reach the EU average of public investment, the German government would have to invest an additional 25 billion Euros per year. The government of Chancellor Angela Merkel so far only committed to the ridiculous amount of 9 billion Euros while continuing to bail out banks and shareholders by hundreds of billions.

Another 50 billion Euros per year should be spent on a future-investment – program focusing on fighting climate change, enhancing infrastructure, transport, education and healthcare which would immediately create a million, new, regular paid and socially secured jobs.

UNLESS THE INCOME DISTRIBUTION IS REVERSED, THERE WON'T BE CURE

The radical re-distribution of income and wealth from bottom to top of society by the neo-liberal agenda especially pursued by social-democratic – green governments in Germany, socialists in France and New Labour in Great-Britain has to be reversed.

Minimum wages, allowances and pensions have to be increased in order to enhance domestic demand. Not tax relief for the rich will increase the social purchasing power that constantly declined during the supposedly "economic good times" as EU currency and economic affairs commissioner Joaquin Almunia always called the past years but the strengthening of middle – and working class.

Low paid and unsecured labour has to be regulated by the state and not by recruitment agencies. Secondary jobs be put under social benefit schemes in order to protect workers.

Again, funds for above should be there as the capital coefficient proves that productivity constantly has risen while social standards and wages declined. It is a mere question of distribution of wealth.

LET THE BENEFICIARIES OF THE PREVIOUS *CASINO KAPUTTALISM* PAY

The financial bubble that burst will be a huge burden for the taxpayers for a long time. It would be logic to ask those to pay who had profited from the previous speculation-parties. A special millionaires-levy for privately owned assets in excess of one million Euros could be a good beginning. In Germany, such a tax at the modest rate of 5% would immediately create 80 billion Euros in revenues. In a country of 80 million people, only some 80,000 would be affected, so just about 1% of the population, the upper class so to speak.

By closing the loopholes for major corporations which have more or less legally laundered their money in the black holes of the financial markets, the various off-shore and tax havens, trillions could be recovered. The World Bank estimates that a quarter of the world's GDP is laundered in the financial off-shore centres.

All the above certainly makes more sense than asking the citizens to tighten their belts again by imposing levies and increasing direct and indirect taxes onto them, or equally insane, to increase tax revenue from SMEs, the backbone of any European economy.

In Germany, 170 billion Euros annually could be repatriated and used for the various stimulus packages and public investments.

Although, all these measurements are absolutely feasible and actually necessary in order to overcome the present crisis it is unlikely that the cartel of neo-liberal parties throughout the EU will walk even one step into this direction. Realistically, one has to see that without pressure from the general public neither EU Commission nor member state governments will stop to listen to the 'elite'.

ANGLO-SAXON MODEL: BECOMING RICH WITHOUT WORKING

No wonder that the Anglo-Saxon financial business model got a bad name: it interfered with other European nation's business interests. As the Anglo-Saxon model is based on the so called *Hedge Funds Industry* that generates money out of hot air and uses such funds to buy-up real economy enterprises across the world, one may understand that some countries do not like to see their industries become subject to takeovers financed by virtual money. Germany only very late, under Social Democratic Chancellor Gerhard Schröder, allowed British and American Hedge Funds to operate in it's territory. France has always maintained a bit more of a protectionist. Especially in the UK this money – spinning "industry" has advanced to the major business and has successively replaced the manufacturing and innovative industries in Great-Britain. Instead, 'smart, young, urban, professionals' generate money without working or without any manufacturing being relevant.

It is comfortable for a nation to lay back and print money while others still work and produce the goods one can import, but it is not a model for the future. In fact, since the Roman Empire, no such system survived in history for long. The decline comes along with a rising brutality, barbarism and degeneration.

Hedge Funds existed in various forms in history but in 1966 they were given their name. Until the end of 2007, the year when the final collapse of our financial system became irreversible, all 9,000 Hedge Funds gambled with about 2.7 trillion Dollars. The top 100 of these betting offices flip over some 1.8 trillion Dollars every day. Most of the Hedge Funds only exist for a few years, more than 60% of them disappear within 3 years. Among the biggest and most well-known are the British MAN Group, JP Morgan Asset Management and Goldman Sachs Asset Management and are directly linked to the broker houses of the same name.

The underlying idea of the hedging is to buy undervalued commercial paper and to simultaneously borrow overvalued and to sell those after a certain time. These transactions can be reversed after a specific time-span making it possible for the Hedge Fund to generate profit entirely independently from the development at the stock market.

Over the decades since 1949 when the first of these transactions had been observed by Fortune Magazine this method has been refined and became ever more sophisticated. But, the speculation is still kind of the same. The classical sense of the term "Hedging" doesn't really apply anymore as it used to be a securitized transaction in which the currency exchange risk was eliminated by buying a certain currency at a fixed price in the future. Today's Hedge Funds don't securitize or insure anything but speculate at the very edge. The effects are usually enhanced by enormous amounts of capital from outside the company, in most cases borrowed funds.

In 1998, the Long Term Capital Management (LTCM) Hedge Fund collapsed as the relation between capital stock and loans has been 1:20. In reality LTCM controlled 5 billion Dollars but traded for 125 billion. When a miss-speculation hit the fund the entire global finance system suddenly was at risk.

The two Hedge Funds which sank the Investment Bank Bear Stearns worked with a ratio of 1:30 meaning that for every Dollar of own capital an additional 30 Dollars of external funds were raised. By employing this tool smallest changes in rates could make huge profits. LTCM indeed managed to realize 40% annual return on investment at the beginning. Usually, Hedge Funds have a certain preference which they speculate in, like so called 'Global Macro Funds' which are betting on changes in the macro-economic field, such as rising or falling exchange rates or the development of interest rates or Hausse or Baisse at the stock market, or even a crash. Even with the latter a lot of money can be earned as we could observe in Summer 2007 when the "Lahnde Capital" hedge fund which had speculated on a devaluation of the sub-prime mortgage papers, so called "Asset Backed Securities" (ABS) that ruined many other Hedge Funds, made miraculously 1000% in profit. It is vitally important to bet on something unpredictable, go against the tide and by this maximize the profit. Or loose, phenomenally, too. It is like on a black jack or Roulette table. Betting on horses is safer as one could at least observe the previous races and conclude from the performance of horse and jockey what the possible result could be. But to conclude that after a rally at the stock markets a period of slower growth would follow could be fatally wrong. It could be the opposite which we have observed during the dotcom bubbles of the Clinton-Gore years and the real estate hype that absorbed a lot of the liquidity when the Clinton-Gore bubbles burst in the wake of September 11.

Another special kind of Hedge Funds are the so called 'vulture funds' which are buying up bad debt or shares of troubled companies aspiring to make more money in the end. Many of the Hedge Funds follow market-neutral strategies by which they spread the risk and are a bit more independent from the general development of the market, i.e. a Hausse or Baisse at the stock market. This usually follows the so called 'long-short – principle'. In this speculative transaction a paper is being bought, in trader-language "the fund goes long" in this transaction. Simultaneously another paper is being borrowed and sold which in trader-language is called "short". After a certain time the paper will be sold again and the borrowed one be re-bought and returned. It is clear that the 'long-position' makes profit if the price for the paper has risen in the meantime while the 'short-position' is beneficial when share prices are falling.

A long-short speculation indeed does make sense if it were in both cases stocks of companies in the same country, of which the one appears to be slightly overvalued while the other seems to be underestimated. All the above is, of course, highly speculative. Although the Hedge Funds only hold little more than 2% of the global investment capital they account for up to 50% of the daily turnover at the global stock markets. More than 15% of the transaction volume of commercial paper and obligations are traded by Hedge Funds. For credit derivatives such as Credit Default Swaps a market share of more than 58% can be noticed. And for Junk Bonds it is still 25%. This shows that the impact of the Hedge Funds on the global markets is much bigger than the actual volume they represent.

The biggest increase of the Hedge Fund 'industry' has been observed since the mid 1990ies. The volume of funds traded through Hedge Funds had multiplied by the factor 1000 since 1995. This has been the result of deregulation of the global financial markets and any liberalisation. In addition to that the wealth of these investors had exploded since the beginning of the 1990ies as 80% of the funds invested in Hedge Funds were owned by High Net-Worth Individuals (HNWIs) who owned at least one million Dollars in cash. But, also the Ultra-High Net-Worth Individuals (UHNWIs) of which there are approximately 100,000 worldwide who by definition can call more than 30 million Dollars in cash deposits their own 'invested' even bigger amounts billion-fold. The remaining 20% of the funds invested in Hedge Funds are stemming from institutional investors such as pension funds which proves that the privatisation of pension systems directly sponsors the most dangerous financial investment vehicles that ruthlessly 'invest' and by this gamble with the social existence of every citizen who trusts in these companies. A very drastic example of how bad things go wrong has been reported from England in 2005 when several companies had told their workers to sign-up for a private pension scheme that later was found to have invested into Hedge Funds and Private Equity firms which used the worker's contributions to buy up shares of those companies the workers were employed by and forcing the management of those companies to maximize the profit by laying people off and cutting down social expenditure. In other words:

the workers faced their own reckoning when putting their signatures under the private pension scheme.

A Pound of Euros, please

February 2009

More then ten years ago, Germany was pushing the UK to join the European Monetary Union (EMU) which resulted in the virtual creation of the Euro as a currency which two years later, on 1 January 2001 began to circulate as legal tender in 10 member states.

At that time Chancellor of the Exchequer Gordon Brown told me in September 1997, so only months after the first election of *New Labour*, that Britain was to transfer most of its gold reserves to Frankfurt in an attempt to at least have a foot in the door although not joining the Euro, yet.

For more than a decade UK politics debated possible scenarios under which 60 years after WWII Great-Britain could economically surrender to Frankfurt.

The scenario which is now likely to make it happen has not been among the ones debated. And, it doesn't seem to be an issue that can be debated for long, if one considers the de-facto declaration of bankruptcy of the British government which had to admit in February 2009 that guarantees by the Bank of England are no longer covered.

Now, as the US will simply inflate their currency and by this get rid of part of their international debts, which will give the US economy a chance to breath, the UK can not revert to same method as the Pound Sterling does not pose as a reserve currency.

But, so does the Euro, even though ECB President Jean-Claude Trichet himself seems not to have fully comprehended this as his appearances in front of the European Parliament's Economic and Monetary Affairs committee suggests.

The UK ought to join either Euro or Dollar as otherwise one can only declare all debts null and void which effectively would be a revolution and start from scratch. This is rather unlikely to happen as it would not only wipe out *New Labour* but would also not leave a subsequent Tory-government with no other choice but nationalisation of key industries. Adam Smith would turn in his grave, Karl Marx laugh.

Chancellor of the Exchequer Alistair Darling thus only has the choice between a bitter apple and a rotten apple.

Germany, although having always pressed for a UK membership in the Frankfurt – Club under present circumstances sees this possibility with rather mixed feelings as it could affect German exports terribly by letting the euro become stronger than ever before.

A SOUND-PROOFED GOVERNMENT

One may wonder these days whether Downing Street is that soundproof. As the BBC reported in March 2009, taxpayer's money committed to bailing out banks and their shareholders has reached 1.3 trillion pounds.

The amount equals the UK's economic annual output. In other words, if the entire workforce and all industries and businesses took a 365 days holiday same damage would be recorded.

That may as well be only the beginning as a confidential paper of the EU Commission has revealed earlier this month.

According to the paper that had been leaked to The Daily Mirror the EU Commission internally assessed that some 18 trillion of poisoned commercial paper is circulating in Europe.

With the City of London being the home of most of the 1,400 hedge funds operating in the EU and any European and international bank it is likely that the figure quoted by the BBC may easily be ten times bigger.

Tragic for the UK as the Anglo-Saxon business model of printing and selling worthless paper has so far accounted for 67% of the UK's GDP.

IT business is to a large degree handled by India, manufacturing by Far East while Britain is totally dependent on imports of raw materials but also food since the agricultural production (1% of British GDP) had been neglected and somehow sacrificed on the altar of EU membership by agreeing to certain quota supposedly designed to counter over-production.

The question put by me to Prime Minister Gordon Brown in October 2008[7] whether Britain would come to ask for aid in Brussels one day if the City was gone could bear a new relevance again.

Irish Lisbon-Referendum Remake

April 2009

It all happened at the same time:

Opinion polls showed the *Fianna Fail* lead Irish government under Taosiaech Brian Cowen trailing opposition parties Fine Gael and Labour for the first time in more than a decade.

A government conducted poll testing the water for a second go on the Lisbon treaty showed for the first time since 13th June 2007 a tiny lead for the 'Yes' campaign although the question had been put in a manipulative way suggesting that changes to the treaty had been made which is a blatant lie.

While the government being under immense pressure by EU institutions and other EU governments to 'deliver' on the Lisbon treaty a scandal broke over the nationalised Anglo-Irish Bank not willing to reveal the names of the "golden circle" ten investors who had been granted loans to buy shares in same bank for which the taxpayer will have to jump in now.

Ireland, after having put the building bubble – based 'Celtic Tiger' to rest, is now facing state bankruptcy of the kind that hit Iceland after the snowball system there collapsed, unless someone jumps to help.

The Price of being on Germany's short list & why the UK is not on it

There is, one hears in Berlin, kind of a shortlist of member states which the German government considers worthwhile to assist overcome the crisis. As the Anglo-Saxon scam artists have sunk *The City* and with it all the useless virtual reality casino – type of speculation it can be expected that Germany will still be creditworthy internationally because it hosts the European Central Bank and still has a broad manufacturing basis.

---

7   Watch it here: www.eureporter.co.uk/

Although it has been pushed for the last 10 years to join the European Monetary Union (EMU) and adopt the Euro, the UK would nowadays not be welcomed with open arms as its tremendous debts would be a huge burden for the single currency which is aspiring global reserve - status after the collapse of the US Dollar.

For Ireland, it may become crucial now to be friendly with Germany but this means to ratify the infamous Lisbon treaty defying worries about militarization, neo-liberal reforms and the creation of a super-state.

Germany, a source close to Chancellor Angela Merkel speaking on condition of anonymity told EUreporter stands ready to buy out Euro-zone countries but will impose strict austerity as "the German public wouldn't understand that we drown taxpayer's money in the Irish Sea".

First indications how said 'austerity' would look can be seen in the Irish government's harsh pension regime involving a 7.5% levy taken from pay cuts of civil servants prompting a day of strike by lower paid civil servants on this week's Thursday under the slogan "Why bailout banks which will repossess our houses?"

A STRONG SHOULDER TO LEAN ON

Despite the fact that the spiral of the EU-wide wage- and standard dumping competition is pointing downwards and many citizens (not only in Ireland) say they fear that this is going to worsen if the Lisbon Treaty came into effect it may well be that during the present crisis the Irish rather want to have a shoulder to lean on.

Although the citizens may not know the exact wording of the framework they obviously had their guts tell them that Articles 49, 54 and 56 of the Lisbon Treaty liberating labour- and services markets will serve for justifications to introduce the lowest standards in terms of wages and social rights they may feel not be left with any choice.

This may as well be true for SME's providing services who all of a sudden are finding themselves competing with companies adhering to lower standards across the EU.

And, at the height of the crisis of the financial markets it may have dawned at citizens that Article 63 of the Lisbon-Treaty which out-rules any regulation, control or overseeing of the flow of capital will ultimately result in the replacement of the profit-oriented creative destruction by the destruction of creativity, productivity and production.

The 'No' campaign this time around was defeated. Some of the fear campaign may have come across as an overkill. Irish voters didn't believe that their freedom would be at stake and that they would lose their independence.

This may be because in reality there is no such thing as a truly independent state. Larger ones always dominate smaller ones. In the case of Ireland it has been for a long time Great-Britain, it now will be the EU in which Germany plays a key role.

Nevertheless, one will find people say that they hate the English for the 800 years of occupation but then cheer their football clubs, copy lifestyle and fashion. Will this shift now to focusing on Germany? Unlikely.

What is more striking is the question what impact the Lisbon treaty is actually going to have on life in the EU.

It is a treaty that has been drafted in a time where the Merry-Go-Round of the financial capitalism was in full swing

It is likely that the Lisbon – Treaty's articles 49, 54 and 56 calling for further liberalisations and deregulations of labour and services markets will serve as justification for an EU – wide wage- and social standards – dumping, but aren't the Irish workers not known for their effective industrial actions? Together with French and other European unionists they can tell their government where the hammer hangs.

This may as well be true for SME's providing services who all of a sudden are finding themselves competing with companies adhering to lower standards across the EU, but will everything fall back on Bulgarian or Romanian or soon Ukrainian standard? Probably not.

It is also amusing to read at the height of the crisis of the Casino Capitalism Article 63 of the Lisbon-Treaty which out-rules any regulation, control or overseeing of the flow of capital. This is clearly an outdated passage of the treaty as well and is overhauled already by various international institutions, the G20, IMF, World bank. And, if those reforms are not sufficient, the system will once more crash and probably disappear or it will ultimately result in the replacement of the profit-oriented creative destruction by the destruction of creativity, productivity and production.

Is the Lisbon treaty adressing this in a relevant way? No. Reality will kick in and teach us what to do, with or without the Lisbon treaty.

The Lisbon treaty has effectively be blown out of the water by governments applying Keynesianism

What is, indeed, worrying is the fact that Article 3 of the treaty allows for unanimous changes that do not have to pass any ratification processes such as a referendum again. We, the citizens, have given our governments a free hand.

VALIDATING THE TICKET BY MAKING IT VOID

July 2009

Since the German federal constitutional court in Karlsruhe had ruled in July 2009 that the Lisbon treaty generally was in line with Germany's *Basic Law*, West-Germany's post WWII constitution, as long as no factual power or German sovereignty was transferred to Brussels, the danger of subordinating national power has become irrelevant. The German constitutional court practically has ruled as only a German court could say it: that the treaty derives it's validity by being declared null and void. It is like tram tickets in Germany becoming valid through cancellation.

This doesn't mean that the Lisbon treaty has no effect at all on German legislation, but it's dimension and it's automatism has been smashed. Although the European Court of Justice based many of it's anti-labour-rights decisions on the Lisbon strategy like when ruling against the *subsidiarity principle* forcing states to allow unsecured labour in carrying out public contracts, from now on no German government can simply shrug it's shoulders and point to Brussels when being confronted by the citizen. No, the German constitutional court ruled that the decisions about the Lisbon treaty's various implementations and their extents have to be made in Berlin, meaning such decisions will have to be dealt with by the German Bundestag, the only parliament Germans should recognise.

Democracy in those member states where national parliaments have a say about the implementation of regulations resulting from the Lisbon treaty will be better protected, that's for sure. Since Czech President Vaclav Klaus gave his signature at the beginning of November 2009 there is nothing stopping the full implementation of the framework any longer. After the Maastricht accord technically having become irrelevant over the financial and economic crisis, the chances are great that the Lisbon treaty can be watered down in the same manner.

The UK's independence party (UKIP) could as well pack up and go home as the European Parliament and EU Commission will ever more be under the shoe of national politics. UKIP did better demand social justice and equality, a fair distribution of wealth, a proper health care system, fair wages and a humane pension scheme in Westminster rather than wasting time, energy and taxpayer's money on campaigning against a paper tiger.

SHALL WE TRUST THEM A FINAL TIME?

March 2009

Recession, depression, it seems to be doom and gloom everywhere. Even those mainstream economists who until recently had justified any of the social cuts or neo-liberal reforms advocated by EU Commission and member state governments, suddenly seem to realise that there were nothing like "economic good times" that EU Currency and Economic Affairs Commissioner Joaquin Almunia celebrated only weeks before. Economists and politicians who created the myth of the self-healing powers of a free market and predicted a long lasting Aufschwung (economic up-swing) for Germany and the euro-zone seem to have been proven wrong. Nevertheless, Czech President Vaclav Klaus writes in the Financial Times under the headline "Do not tie the markets – free them" that "we have to weaken labour, environmental, social, health and other 'standards' that block rational human activity". Does this man read a paper or watch TV, one might wish to ask.

The German economy is predicted to shrink by 4% in 2009, the US crashed already by 5.1% in the last quarter of 2008 despite all statistical tricks the North Americans traditionally apply. But, also the emerging economies such as India and China are stagnating at best. The international banking system has dried up while an incredible liquidity bubble of debts is hanging over the global economy and threatening to create a financial tsunami wiping out entire economies if it is dropped. These debts were created by Jedi Riders in the virtual reality casino of the financial markets and by those mainstream economists and politicians who rolled out the red carpet for Hedge Fund junkies and Private Equity sharks by granting tax relief, deregulating markets and cutting labour costs and social rights. Now, the same crooks try to make the world believe that they will finally get it right and fix the problem by Keynesian tools and stimulus packages. Are we going to trust them one last time?

AMERICANS TO WAKE UP TO A COUNTRY PLASTERED WITH FOOD-STAMPS

The EU27 current account deficit in the third quarter of 2008 was 39.5 billion Euros - in 2007 it was only 9.7 billion. Industrial new orders in the euro-zone are down by 4.5% in November 2008 compared with October 2008. In the EU27 it was 3.9% so not even cheap labour and poor social standards in Eastern European member states can save us. The euro-zone's unemployment rate in December 2008 was up to 8%, in the EU27 up to 7.4%, in December 2007 it was around 7%. A drastic increase is predicted for 2009. In the US, 2 million people lost their jobs in the past 4 months while 3 million employees were pushed into secondary jobs and further job losses of some 5 million are expected. Meanwhile, 31.5 million Americans in September 2008 were reliant on food stamps - as many as ever before since its introduction on which people rely to avoid starvation, since the Clinton administration has limited social security benefits to 5 years per person and per life. Despite these dramatic statistics, governments across the Atlantic as well as here in Europe appear to be eager to ease the effects of the economic collapse by so called 'stimulus packages'. But, will these really work?

If one scrutinizes the various stimulus packages there is no such thing as a diametrically opposed approach many commentators want to make us believe. All these nationalisations are not ending in a directed economy at all but in re-privatisations after the public have swallowed the debts. Our politicians are still serving the same ruler, although said fat rich ruler now is weak and suffering from anorexia and would need good care and tea rather than wild parties and buyable love.

SOCIALISM FOR BANKERS

In other words: whilst yesterday it was the free market that guaranteed the upper class's exploding income to finance its excesses, it is now the state that is needed to protect their assets which had been accumulated by gambling rather than any wise investment decision. Of course, these people and their acolytes, who for decades had called for a lean state, now advocate "big is beautiful". Billions are currently pumped into an ailing economy but our political leaders wouldn't dare to ask the beneficiaries of the previous economic insanity to donate a few cents from their exorbitant gains. Instead, most governments debate granting further tax relief which, because of its progressive nature, ensures that the rich benefit much more than those on lower incomes. This will not stimulate domestic demand as Eurostat's household savings rate projection proves, pointing upwards again (14.4% in euro-zone and 10.7% in EU27)[8] partly because investments from volatile financing schemes are withdrawn and put on ordinary savings accounts and partly because banks are not handing out loans anymore. And, for 80% of society the savings rate declines for quite some time already, not of course this is not so for the upper quintile. The additional funds gained from tax relief are certainly not invested and probably also not used for increasing consumption but kept in savings accounts. At the same time our political leaders continue to preach water while they and theirs drink wine: demand would be there but is killed off by the absence of real purchasing power due to shrinking wages, poor social standards and pensions. People would love to consume but they aren't given the funds …

---

8   Financial Times 7th January 2009
     Eurostat releases 11, 12, 13, 14/2009 30th January 2009

SHAREHOLDER'S FRIEND

In Berlin, Washington, Tokyo and Beijing enormous amounts are pumped into the real economy but the effects are rather marginal. The black hole of the financial market still sucks and creates further bubbles by debt. US President Barack Obama pushed a stimulus package of 825 billion Dollars through Congress and Senate topping it up to 890 billion. In China it will be 580 billion Dollars and in Japan 100 billion Dollars that shall miraculously spur the economy. Great Britain so far spent £20 billion, France 26 billion Euros, Germany €50 billion, but these packages mostly consist of measures that had been planned for quite some time. Most creatively the Italian government vigorously fought against the crisis by announcing a €80 billion stimulus package but its core is actually only 6 billion. (The first German stimulus package was said to be €30 billion, in reality it was little more than a third of that. It is, of course, election time in Germany.)

The most practical and fastest way to enhance domestic demand and to bolster the economy would be a radical re-distribution of income and wealth from top to bottom of society. Socially just economics are the only viable response to the crisis. The fact that this is widely ignored proves that the stimulus packages of our governments are not intended to really fight the crisis and prevent the collapse of our economic system, but to stabilise and maintain the wealth distribution that shall ensure future profits of the elites, and to protect their income and wealth. The contradiction between increased demand and profit interests dominates all stimulus packages of the past months. The task for those packages is not only to create demand but to make sure that this doesn't harm the capital accumulation. That's not to be done easily. Major components of the various stimulus packages are public investments, direct help for ailing industries by state guarantees and cash injections and an increase of private consumption. But will this really help? The American stimulus package contains a $275 billion in tax relief which the Senate wants to increase by another 70 billion. Low income families, the unemployed, and working families on average incomes who would need a stimulus most, won't see much of it which makes these packages quite useless. But, tax relief has always been in the neo-liberal's text books. The momentum of a crisis is a good way to push through what hasn't worked in normal times.

RIDICULOUS IMPERTINENCE…

In Germany, for instance, the tax relief granted will amount to €150 million for people earning less than €10,000 a year, but €1.45 billion (ten times more!) for those who earn more than €53,000 per annum. This may be a comforting thought for the rich in times of crashing stock markets but other than that, nothing will be won by these tax relief packages. A special way of granting tax relief has been tested in Great Britain by reducing VAT by 2.5%. Because indirect taxes always bear a regressive effect, such a move might appeal at first sight. But, the VAT reduction is not passed on to the consumer but is used by retailers and industry to fiddle their balance sheets. Downing Street now understands the folly of this adventure that will cost 14 billion in 2009. Also, the consumption checks sent out by the Japanese and French governments will not really help as these will be one-time effects designed to ignite a little firework. A worldwide economic crisis won't be overcome by this. That's probably why the new US administration doesn't waste a second thought on that. Predecessor George W. Bush's efforts in December 2008 had almost no effect. Also, President Obama's pledge to increase unemployment benefits and health care spending won't undo the impertinent income distribution of the past decades. Especially between 2001 and today 96% of all income increases in the US benefited the richest 10% of society. They won't be able to bring things back on track as they won't increase their spending significantly.

Suddenly multinational corporations perfectly know which national government to revert to in order to ask for bail-out. Formerly 'globalized' industries become patriotic.

Last but not least, the idea to support industries by cash injections without taking control of the companies only further cements the ridiculous income and wealth distribution patterns of the past. It will always be more expensive to finance a lifeline for the owners of ailing industries, than to finance production and work places in a publicly owned company. In the latter case one would first use up all available capital including privately held stock of the company in order to cover its debt prior to the state dig deep in his pocket. In that case one would only have to finance the production and wages but no shareholder value. This will be the only way to make sure that the capital accumulation insanity doesn't start anew. To grant rich shareholders tax relief while financing the losses of stock listed companies with public money is as crazy as creating publicly financed dumps for commercial paper trash of the financial institutions. The interest-driven background of these stimulus packages is to be witnessed in the absurd protectionism that evaporates at every major multinational corporation these days. The same people who were singing the globalisation hymn all along now know quite well which state they have to revert to in order to have their shareholder value rescued.

If one wants to spend a lot of money one either has to make a lot of money or take out loans. All governments presently favour the latter. The US government expects a deficit of $1.2 trillion, more than 8% of the country's GNP. Europe doesn't perform much better. Although the Maastricht accord behind which the neo-liberal austerity fanatics were hiding for the past 15 years calls for a 3% (of GNP) ceiling for public debt, Ireland expects it to be 11% this year and 13%. The next France (5.4%) and Spain (6.2%) are topping Germany, which expects it to be 4 or 5% in this year.

It wouldn't be a catastrophe if the Maastricht accord finally were to be buried, but excessive public debt is also no good sign even if it is paid back to the last euro, because also public debts can not be extended indefinitely either without ending in bankruptcy. But, those huge debts are likely to be used as an excuse for a new drive for austerity and wage 'moderation' and brutal cuts in the social-, health care-, educational and environmental field. The only alternative would be to let those pay for the previous party who profited from it. Let's present the bill. It could be a millionaires levy, or a tax on financial transactions but this seems to be not politically feasible as long as the insight of the ruling politicians probably will only be helped by pressure by those who they rule over. The general strike of 29 January in France could mark a new beginning. We will almost certainly see much more of these actions across Europe and maybe even in the US once our friends across the Atlantic have woken up to a country plastered by food stamps.

WHISTLING IN THE WOODS

March 2009

A day after the EU finance ministers passed another watery resolution to combat the financial crisis by regulating a bit here and there, ECB – President Jean-Claude Trichet reiterated that financial institutions and hedge funds especially needed to be supervised.

"This has to be applied also and foremost to the trading with derivatives." Mr. Trichet said departing from his long-time stance of only "observing and analysing what was going on with those very sophisticated instruments"[9].

In lieu of the fact that the financial crisis has brought down the real economy in almost every corner of this planet the initiatives of European Central Bank and EU member state governments of which the most important ones had met over the weekend in Berlin, the measurements can be described as 'too little – too late'.

More transparency and control alone won't help the economy which Deutsche Bank AG sees collapse by more than 5% in Germany in 2009 while the German government officially still speaks of 2.5% back on track.

The most important question would be why the EU's institutions as well as the member state governments have not shut down tax havens by denying their banks and major corporations to operate in those off-shore centres a long time ago? Warning signs had been there plenty well before the credit crunch.

Financial direct investment into the EU had doubled between 2006 and 2007 meaning that major corporations and banks had more or less legally laundered their profits under palm trees and re-injected those into the EU.

This has not been a new development and certainly has not come as a surprise as even Economic Affairs Commissioner Joaquin Almunia had to admit when asked by EUreporter in November 2007.

---

9   ECB-president Jean-Claude Trichet at the Davos Economic Forum 2007
    according to Financial Times

HAS IT BEEN TRUE WHAT THEY TOLD US BACK THEN?

And, how can it be that banks which are now reliant on state aid still helped their most privileged clients to evade taxes by shuffling away billions? Or why is it still possible for banks to pay shareholders huge dividends despite tremendous losses? Why are their still discussions about manager bonuses if only losses are recorded? And why are hedge funds still legal and not banned from operating in the EU?

Meanwhile, the EU Commission seems to be further sidelined as member states are increasingly often act without consulting or even retrospectively informing the Brussels based institution.

Also, the latest attempt by EU Commission president José Manuel Barroso to propose a 5 billion Euros stimulus package for energy projects was rebuffed by EU foreign ministers. Not that its size would come along as a joke anyhow, it anyway would only pour money in an over-financed market potentially creating another bubble for climate change - junkies who need a new playground for their billions after the building bubbles in Bulgaria, Spain, Ireland and other states has let the air off by scam artists.

If one really wanted to construct a new, crisis resistant, world financial system one could have posed as a good example by applying real measurements that would have an immediate effect in the European Union rather than engaging in half-hearted micro-reforms which do not resonate more than whistling in the woods.

NOT ONLY US'S FAULT

The global reserve system urgently needs to be reformed with the United States having accumulated a deficit of more than 850 billion Dollars and adding another 700 billion Dollars by the bailout bill on Thursday, 2nd October 2008. It won't be the American taxpayers who will pay for it, it is everyone who buys US government obligations.

China instead accounts for a surplus of 150 billions. A good deal of the blame for the financial crisis can be put down to the fact that the Dollar has been *the* global reserve currency. For some time already it is rivalled by the euro. The question whether the euro as the supposedly more stable currency should replace the Dollar is at hand, but would that be feasible?

China is not the only creditor to the United States. In a way, many countries, including those of the so called "third world" made the continuation of the American bubble-building possible. The tragedy lies in the fact that these poor and emerging countries are both, suffering from any economic downturn in the US while at the same time being forced to contribute to the bubble building by buying US treasury bonds.

Higher savings than investment opportunities in the rest of the world led to an uninterrupted flow of capital to the US. The so called recycling of Petro-Dollars rose from 6-8% of GDP to over 30% of the GDP in 2007 while the demand of Dollar reserves as a result of increased trade in emerging markets and at the same time increasing volatility and now the worldwide financial crisis let this bubble further swallow.

Especially in emerging markets the demand for Dollar reserves go up by billions. Governments of these countries (like India, Brazil and others) want to protect their sovereignty and not be stripped off it by the IMF and therefore create Dollar reserves. In a way so called "third world" countries are lending to the United States and by this are contributing to the ongoing craziness of feeding bubble over bubble.

Economic Nobel Prize winner Professor Joseph Stiglitz told me at the International Economists Association conference in Istanbul that because fiscal deficits in the U.S. were endogenous and because foreigners wanted to hold T-bills in reserves the exchange rate needed to be adjusted to make it possible which sounds absolutely logic since the reason for the declining Dollar is not the demand for US American goods by foreign countries that shall be encouraged.

The Dollar depreciation is seen as a good environment to compensate debt by foreign currency. "At first glance this may appeal but the reality is that the US as well as the rest of the world would be better off shifting to a global reserve currency" Professor Stiglitz concluded.

The fact that the U.S. economy is suffocating because of hyperventilation from all the extra liquidity been thrown by the international community at the U.S. for building US Dollar reserves amid the spreading crisis not only leads to inflation in the U.S. but also cripples the economy as the bubble building is fed, not a Hausse which would be so badly needed.

Professor Stiglitz puts it bluntly: "Surplus countries are as much part of the systematic un-sustainability which is not in the interest of the United States" as it is not in the interest of borrowers who think that "they avail of low interest loans although the US is loosing from high instability and exporting T-bills". And, he added "the current system is inherently unsustainable" leading to an "unstable process and risk of crisis that drives up demand for reserves". Nothing, the Europeans should wish to inherit if the euro is to become the new global reserve currency one may think.

A SENSE OF DISSOLUTION

EU Competition Commissioner Neelie Kroes complained that she had not been informed by the German government about it's bail-out of Hypo Real Estate Group (HRE). At a press conference following the dramatic weekend in September 2008 Mrs. Kroes urged member state governments to "please pick up the telephone and call us". What may appear to sound overly dramatic lays bare that despite all efforts to find a common European answer to the financial crisis, member states still act on national level while ignoring EU regulations completely.

That EU institutions are not functioning as planned during the crisis became clear at the press conference of EU Internal Market Commissioner Charlie McCreevy an hour later during which the commissioner unveiled his plans for tougher bank regulation, the so called 'Capital Requirements Directive'. Under the new rules, banks will be forced to retain capital for at least 5% of the exposures they securitize.

It will not take more than a few risk calculations for banks and insurance companies to figure out how much money they can make with the 95% of trading potential whereas the risk to loose 5% if it goes wrong is relative minimal. Commissioner McCreevy admitted that he would like to have seen a much higher rate of 15% or at least 10% but because banks opposed this he could not get support for this in the EU Commission.

The proposed directive also does not include any regulations concerning Hedge Funds and Private Equity firms although the Rasmussen – report passed by the European Parliament winning an overwhelming majority a week before, called in particular for such.

The question may be asked how many more banks need to crash before the existing financial market policy of the EU will be adjusted. Commissioners Kroes and McCreevy both avoid such debate as it inevitably would lead to the question what use in terms of real economic growth the construction of hyper-complex financial instruments which risk factor no investor is able to assess are of. The only sensible reaction might be to ban the trading of credit obligations and derivatives as such obviously can not function in a safe way while on the other hand bearing the potential of doing serious harm to our economies.

The personal background of both commissioners who in their careers had either been on boards of banks or lobbied for such also became a matter of discussions.

Meanwhile, EU Commission president José Manuel Barroso at his press conference demanded an international conference on the financial crisis lauding the European Central Bank for it's wise role in keeping the markets afloat: "I would underline in particular that this is working well not only at the national level but also at cross border level" the Commission president emphasised.

The reality rather seems to be very different: Governments ignore EU Commission, EU Commission ignores European Parliament, the European Parliament fails to review it's own spending and keeps on trucking having film festivals and parties in it's buildings so what shall the citizen take from that?

Not Everybody's Darling

Prime Minister Gordon Brown and Chancellor of the Exchequer Alistair Darling in slashing VAT undermine EU tax harmonisation. Continental governments are upset by the move of Great-Britain. After the Irish government's undercutting of European banking bail-out by unilaterally guaranteeing for banks the Labour government's push to lower VAT in the UK to the mandatory minimum 15% comes as the second major blow to European integration.

While the German government is still debating on how to salvage its heavily affected economy by small tax breaks such as vehicle registration fees and motor tax, the British government simply did it.

Tax harmonisation has always been an issue vigorously been fought over in Europe. Germany's approach has been to harmonise VAT. The share of corporate and income tax in the overall revenue of Germany has steadily declined for the past 25 years while the contributions to the overall tax budget made from indirect taxes as well as VAT have doubled.

The German government has gradually raised VAT in order to make good on the de-flux of corporate and income tax which were lowered in a tax-dumping style of competition with other European member states like Ireland, the UK and several Eastern European countries.

All what the European Parliament could agree on this year was VAT harmonisation. Corporate – and income taxes were – for a good reason – left out of the equation as ultra rich and major corporations fiercely resisted any further harmonisation in this field.

Now, as the European common market allows citizens to buy goods in any of the 27 member states and can easily do so even from home by Tele-shopping or by ordering through internet retailers, the British undercutting of VAT will seriously affect other European economies.

Germany and other continental European governments won't like Chancellor of the Exchequer Alistair Darling's approach.

Not only comes this as a major blow to European integration but will also be seen as a selfish act of a country's government which has ever since been seen as wearing two hats when it came to EU affairs.

New Labour had, since it was voted in the first time in 1997, taken a pro-European stance and even transferred 2/3 of the UK's gold reserves to the Frankfurt based Bundesbank in an attempt to reassure the continental Europeans of their commitment.

By not joining the European Monetary Union (EMU) in 1999 which led to the introduction of the euro as single currency it has been clear that if Britain was to join at a later stage the terms and conditions would be different.

Most of the European Central Bank's staff was recruited from former Bundesbank officials. In order to keep at least a foot in the door the British government was betting on being allowed a special status.

Nevertheless, over the years it has become more and more unlikely that more than 60 years after WWII Britain would 'surrender' to Frankfurt.

Now, as the Budget has been approved by the House of Commons, it has become clear that inadvertently the Labour government has kissed its European commitment good-bye.

A Belgian citizen, André, to who I spoke when the news broke commented: "The British are with one foot in Europe and with one in America."

But, one should add, what will happen to the foot they left in the door of the European Central Bank?!

IV.

METHODOLOGICAL INSANITY

Early cycles of concurring Capitalism

"In order to maintain the prices the state had to pay the pre-panic prices and to discount promissory notes which didn't represent anything else but foreign bankruptcies. In other words, the entire wealth of society which the government represents has to compensate the private capitalist's losses. This kind of Communism which mutuality is completely unilateral seems to be quite appealing to the European capitalists."
Karl Marx 'Financial Crisis in Europe' 1857

In a, under humanitarian aspects, barbaric but undoubtedly growth and productivity enhancing way capitalism in it's early days swivelled from upswing to crisis, back and forth. This is the capitalism Adam Smith and Karl Marx defined and described. Back then it has been mostly the investment dynamism which produced an upswing which led to an increased employment, greater profit rates, ever more consumption and, just before the boom peaked, also to higher wages.

Just, when the ever more enhanced capacities created by such a prosperous economy started to produce as well, it became clear that it were too many so that the willingness to invest got slowed down which resulted in an even greater lead of supply over demand.

At this point, back then, as it is today, prices started to fall. This let the purchasing power of the wages go through the roof while profit share rapidly declined bringing any investment cycle to an end.

Companies accounting for a below-average productivity and outdated machines were forced into bankruptcy by this eliminating those overcapacities. Overall, production reached a higher technological level and new inventions and products posed as interesting investment opportunities again.

THE GAME STARTED ALL OVER AGAIN

Until short before the end of the 19th century capitalism followed this pattern of cycles which pretty exactly every ten years ended in crisis. Because the imbalances that could build up during those ten year cycles were kind of limited, the cleaning thunderstorms were not lasting too long either.

This model worked well as long as the competition was well and alive and the market dominance of a single company relatively small. That changed towards the end of the 19th century significantly allowing for the first time ever a globalising capitalism consisting of a free movement of capital along with internationally fit big companies which dominated their domestic market. These *global players* had the privilege to be able to dictate prices, level of wages and political agendas in their home countries.

The main reason for this dominance has not been the lack of regulation to avoid creation of cartels but rather new automated production lines in heavy- and car industry which because of the extremely high capital requirements could never be managed by smaller companies.

As a consequence of the new order the economic dynamism significantly calmed down. In addition the way for economic expansion more and more intensively got paved by political and military power and not technological superiority.

Simultaneously, the income distribution threw up huge imbalances while an ever more aggressive speculation on stock- and financial markets resulted in the Great Depression of the 1930ies. The domestic as well as worldwide economic imbalances which had been accumulated since the turn of the century and especially in the aftermath of WWI rained down in form of WWII - bombs.

The times of Adam Smith and Karl Marx are long gone. Although in his analysis Karl Marx may be unbeaten as after 1989 only capitalistic major corporations behaved in exactly the way he had predicted it can hardly be seen as the future of European economy as we all still remember how the first Socialistic experiment ended in disaster 20 years ago. On the other hand, there can't be any continuation of the kind of capitalism we had seen until last week.

A MATTER OF PRINCIPAL: ZERO IS *NOT* 1!!!

Although IMF, G8, EU as well as the new economic superpowers, India and China, unanimously vowed to stand together in solving the financial crisis, the success of the hundreds of billions heavy rescue packages will be short-lived.

The reasons why there is no cure to the disease our present economic system is suffering from are much deeper rooted:

It is mathematically incoherent. In order to be able to record destruction as 'growth' the neo-classical model set's the axiom $\partial F(x)/\partial x = 0$. If it was $\partial F(x)/\partial x = 1$ this would mathematically mean that the function isn't a continuum. But, in the neo classical economy one wants to uphold the theory that the relations investment-wage, capital & labour, production and productivity, growth and consumption are continuing functions and for this reason set the axiom $\partial F(x)/\partial x = 0$.

NEO-CLASSICAL MODEL TO FAKE MATHEMATICS TO MAKE IT LOOK SOUND

This allows the economic model to substitute factors like 'capital' and 'labour' by whatever figures and assume that it is divisible. The neo-classical model in it's entirety bases on this assumption, making it possible that this model – in theory – shows even then growth rates if consumption declines because of shrinking wages leading to retracting production cycles while the profit rate increases amid declining production output.

Applying this model means that in theory even destruction would be measured as growth. But, the theorists of the neo classical model can't trick mathematics. The function $\partial F(x)/\partial x$ per se can not be a continuous one, only if one set it "0" but that defies any logic as non-continuous functions can not be differentiated.

The manipulated econometrics used by EU Commission, all member states and being taught at most universities also allows to declare the accumulation of wealth outside the production cycle and outside of the control of central banks irrelevant. According to the neo-classical ideology all the bubbles created by the financial market's chain-letter system wouldn't exist.

It has become obvious in the current crisis that a deregulated and liberalised global financial system had enjoyed the privilege of almost without limitation creating credit based funds. Under these circumstances central banks had almost no influence on the capital accumulation as well as the irrational movement and use of such liquidity.

Unfortunately, the system is led ad absurdum. It can't be rescued by liquidity-injections, it's painful decline can only be prolonged. No wonder, that banks from East Asia to Frankfurt and New York celebrated to be given new tokens as it enables them to let it go into the next round. The next crashes, though, are already pre-programmed.

The only way out would be to abandon budget discipline, fiscal austerity and the entire 'Lisbon Strategy of Stability and Growth' and instead drastically increase wages, subsidize producing industries and SMEs especially.

Parallel to this one should re-install currency control mechanisms and ban financial speculation by declaring trading of financial instruments such as derivatives, Commercial Debt Obligations, Mortgage Backed Securities and any equivalent illegal. Then, one also has to return to sound economic models that do not need to bend mathematical rules.

Anything less radical won't help.

The question that arises is a fundamental one. There is no grey area. It is only black or white. Digital, like zero and one. Scientifically it is clear why the financial capitalism couldn't work at all as the neoclassical economic model rests on false assumptions and fatally wrong theories which can only be covered up by manipulating statistics as well as mathematics itself. The impertinent theft by investment banks such as

Goldman Sachs, and Citigroup paying bonuses to their managers out of taxpayer's rescue funds is only a symptom not the cause of the crisis that shall distract our attention away from the real beneficiaries, rich shareholders and owners. A *Third Way* notoriously advocated by Anti Globalization groups and other Green-Social Democratic politicians who rather stand for a certain life-style making us feel good in showing solidarity with the so called '*Third World*' by granting 'debt relief' through our singers Bono of U2 and Bob Geldof, by committing to fighting climate change by fuelling our cars with 'bio-fuel' and by eating overpriced organic food regardless of the fact that we are executing Eco-Fascism won't be the cure to the present crisis. The reason why uprisings are unlikely despite an outrageous income disparity is that we all have been caught by consumerism that silences the masses.

INFLATING DEATH IN SO-CALLED „THIRD WORLD"

Based on the EU's approach towards Asian, Pacific and Caribbean (APC) as well as developing countries means that member states were manipulating their books by calling debt relief, generously granted in 2006, an increase of aid, whereas in reality, the figures are declining: in 2007 it was 46.1 billion while in 2006 it was still 47.7 billion Euros according to Louis Michel, the Commissioner responsible for Development and Humanitarian Aid. This prompted EU Commission president Jose Manuel Barroso on 4th April 2008 to call on member states to increase development aid: "We are worried about this trend because we can not afford to reduce development aid while trying to achieve the UN Millennium Development Goals (MDG)." The background to this is the OECD report citing, for the second year in row, declining figures of global aid bringing it down to a total of 70 billion Euros. In 2005, the EU Council decided to increase aid levels collectively and individually by all member states. The heads of government and states certainly did not have on their minds to use the writing – off of bad loans to the poorest nations as a replacement for their real humanitarian aid packages. Nevertheless, capital transfer from the poorest countries to the rich is ever increasing and the "bad" loans are in multiple ways amortised. Brazil in the 1990ies repaid some 650 billion US Dollars (including interest!) in 2005 again the country was indebted by some 300 billion US Dollars although no new loans had been granted. In a way, these countries, as well as every little dictatorial so-called "Third World" state which is forced to pay back in US Dollars are contributing to the financing of the US's bubbles. In this sense the question of who is granting 'aid' to who needs to be re-examined. The noble attempt of EU Commission president Jose Manuel Barroso and Commissioner Louis Michel to force EU member states to increase their aid is a bit hypocritical as it is the economic system that they uphold that cements this world order financially. At the same time that this cynicism is going on, food prices are soaring, not only in the EU where it simply means that some of us eat less vegetables, fruits and pasta replacing our usual healthy diet with less expensive food, but much more drastically in developing countries where it becomes a question of life and death. Bread in Egypt is 35% more expensive, the price for corn in Mexico has risen by some 50% since US refine it to make bio-fuel from it.

EU PROTECTIONISM AND SUBSIDIES UNDERMINE FREE MARKET

In addition to that in wars more people die through weapons than by starvation. The goal of the UN Millennium summit to halve the amount of hungry people could very cynically be understood in a way that the wars do the job.

The EU's export to APC and developing countries is massively subsidised and by this undermines the agricultural competition in those countries.

On the other hand, our EU market is not fully open to imports from APC countries as huge subsidies are paid from the EU commission to the Agra sector. Biggest beneficiaries are major food corporations and owners of large amounts of agricultural land as an article in the Frankfurter Allgemeine Zeitung[10] describes. As an internal paper of the German government shows, the 30 largest receivers of export subsidies in 2001 had received some 113 million Euros from the EU's agricultural budget. According to the FAZ article the Bonn based Meat

---

10   Frankfurter Allgemeine Zeitung (FAZ) 15th March 2006

Ex- and Import (Bonn Fleisch Ex-und Import GmbH) received 12.8 million Euros, the Nordmilch GmbH 11.7 million Euros and the Swiss company NESTLE 2.4 million Euros. Industrialised countries subsidise their agricultural sectors with 1 billion Dollars per day and create dumping situations on the world market.

All this indicates that we still set the priorities in protecting our own business rather than helping poor and developing countries. That's why the richest Fifth of the world account for 86% of the World GDP while the poorest Fifth only have a 1% share of this planet's economic output. One billion people are homeless, more than 1.5 billion people do not have access to clean, consumable water, 850 million can neither read nor write, 1.3 billion people live on less than 1 $ per day while the three richest human beings own and control a stock of capital that is greater than the total GDP of the 50 poorest countries with their 600 million inhabitants. The world's total spending on arms in 2002 were 794 billion US Dollars and in 2007 already more than a trillion. Despite a permanent net transfer from poor to rich countries the total indebtedness of the developing countries has exploded from 600 billion US Dollars in 1980 to 3.2 trillion US Dollars in 2006. According to the World Bank developing countries are paying 370 billion US Dollars each year for serving the loans.

Since the end of the 1980ies, exactly after the Eastern European Socialism had collapsed and the neo-classical economic model celebrated a revival, the World Bank made privatisations mandatory for obtaining credit from IMF and World Bank. Especially loans granted for water projects were only paid out if those projects were privately controlled. Governments who wish to benefit from the HIPC initiatives for debt write-offs have to present a national fight-poverty – strategy which has to be approved by IMF and World Bank. In 27 of these 43 "Poverty Reduction Strategies" privatisation of water sectors are demanded. This way, a Third of all World Bank loans directly go to privately owned companies, most of these multinationals. An example to where the IMF structural programs lead to can be observed in Zambia. The previously free healthcare for poor people has become unaffordable. The agricultural sector was revamped to become an exporting industry while the basic subsistence for the own population has been totally neglected. Since 1975 the per capita income has fallen by 60%. The loans of the IMF were also made dependent on the privatisation of the mining industry of the country. These privatisations had not positive effects at all. The Committee for Academic Freedom in Africa reported that the World Bank programs had drastic consequences on the educational system in Africa as many governments were forced to introduce school fees. Results were sharply declining school enrolments. Thousands of teachers and students who protested against the new rules were killed.[11] The World Bank admitted in 2000 that the average per capita income in Africa was in 2000 lower than during the independence movements 40 years before while the share of Africa on world trade has halved and now only amounts to two per cent. Some 80% of the population is poor, 20% live in war zones, one in 5 persons is HIV positive and more than 50% have access to clean water while only a third of the total population on that continent has access to healthcare. Just little more than half of the African population can read and write. The entire continent has less many roads than Poland.[12] And, UNICEF reported[13] that 40 years ago the income difference between poorest and richest fifth of the world population has been 1:30 but until 1997 the gulf between rich and poor reached a horrible ratio of 1:78. According to a report of the UN[14] 815 million people were starving, of which 777 million were living in developing countries and 27 million in former Soviet Union countries. In 2000 36 million people died of hunger, of which 7 million were children. On the other side, there are 358 multi-billionaires who own and control of what half of the world population owns. A third of total world trade is conducted by transnational major corporations. More and more investments which destroy employment are made, i.e. in 2005 some 92% of all worldwide foreign direct investments are done in connection with mergers and takeovers. Between 1987 and 2005, the average ratio has been 60.8% per annum. Of the ten largest industrial multinationals 6 are oil companies. 45 of the top 100 companies in the world are financial corporations. More than 50% of the balance of the 50 largest European corporations is accounted for by British and German companies. The 30 DAX corporations control

---

11 Neues Deutschland (ND) 23rd September 2000
12 Frankfurter Allgemeine Zeitung (FAZ) 08th June 2006
13 Frankfurter Allgemeine Zeitung (FAZ) 14th December 1999
14 United Nations FAO report published in Berliner Zeitung 16th October 2001

some 4,500 companies worldwide. All empirical studies prove that the concentration in the financial and banking sector leads to interest increases. This concentration cripples our economies.

FINALLY, SOMEONE TALKS TRUTH ABOUT WORLD BANK

Under the headline "World Bank Report faults bias toward deregulation"[15] the International Herald Tribune published an article about the findings of an investigation into the practices of the World Bank. The article describes that "World Bank's flagship effort to encourage poor nations to slash business regulation is deeply flawed, the bank's in-house watchdog reported, reflecting a growing divide within the bank about how best to boost development." A bit later, the article outlines what is going on in the private sector – department of the World Bank:

"Since 2003, the banks private sector arm the International Finance Corp. has produced an annual series of indicators ranking countries on the ease of doing business getting credit, laying-off workers and registering property. Countries vie to become one of the 'doing business' report's 'top reformers' by slashing regulations and rewriting laws in a way that boosts their rankings. Last year, Egypt used its top reformer status as part of a pitch for more investment abroad and as a re-enforcement for policy makers who want to hack away at decades of regulations from Egypt's socialist past." If that was not enough, the report cites a climate of obedience towards the economic system:

"Developing nations compete with each other to move up on the rankings of 178 nations, figuring that a better ranking will mean additional investment and, ultimately, economic growth (…) But, a critique by the bank's Internal Evaluation Group, which doesn't report to the bank's management, said the Doing Business survey is biased toward deregulation and hypes its results (…) For instance, countries get good marks if it is easier to lay off workers, because the IFC figures employers will be quicker to hire staff if they know they are not stuck with them during downturns." Really an eye opener is the following passage:

---

15   Bob Davis in the International Herald Tribune (IHT) 16th June 2008

"But many poor countries have grown sceptical of market-oriented solutions, feeling that they have mostly helped elites in rich and poor nations.

The bank now is working on similar indicators to rank countries on how well they are reforming their farm sectors."

Well, we have seen already that in the end only those countries who are willing to starve their citizens to death and surrender all wheat and corn to Energy corporations of Western Free Democracies for their bio-fuel production will qualify for World Bank investment ratings!

DEBT RELIEF FOR THE G8

When one hears about the G 8 and their "commitment to help" the poorest countries in the world by a debt relief, one may be tempted to think that Bono, Bob Geldof and Herbert Grönemeyer are doing the right thing to demand that the rich world is writing off the bad debts, like if you can not pay your credit card bills and just avoid insolvency by settling for a minimum amount with your bank while the remainder is generously written off, meaning in the end written off the taxes of the financial institution which socialises its losses, so in the end all consumers pay your debts. But is that really so? A closer scrutiny reveals that not the poor countries owe to the rich but vice versa. In order to understand why the singers should at their "LIVE8" concerts rather call for a debt relief for the rich, industrialized countries one has to have a look at the history of the IMF and World Bank.

The G 8 is since more than 30 years actively pursuing the interest of their various countries' industries against the will and resistance of billions of people, especially in the so called "Third World". It can hardly be seen as a contradiction that emerging economies such as India and China are now also invited to those meetings. It only shows that it becomes more and more difficult for the G8 to maintain an economic regime based on exploitation and violence. An economic system that is directly responsible for the deaths of tens of thousands of people while a billion of our planet's citizens have no access to clean water and are degraded to be seen as 'cost factors' as their social and human rights are trampled on by a small minority becoming richer and richer is faced with an eroding acceptance and diminished moral legitimacy and therefore can much easier be rivalled from emerging economies such as India and China. This is also because it is more and more difficult for the Western Free Democracies to force their former colonies to surrender their natural resources even not by military force as we can see in the case of Afghanistan, Iraq, Somalia and Sudan, the latter also China has an interest in as well since it's booming state-capitalistic economy developed a certain hunger for resources. One can even speak of a proxy war between China and "the West" as the "People's Republic" finances and supports the so called "Islamic Courts" which the "Anti-Terror Fighters of the West" try to eliminate by fighting against "al Qaeda" the "Human Right's Warriors" Bush and Blair were sighting wherever there was an economic interest. And, China doesn't listen to Western World criticism over 'human rights' any longer as it is also major corporations of the 'Western Free Democracies' who entertain production lines in the child labour markets by this ruining the prices back home making it impossible for Small & Medium Sized Entrepreneurs (SME's) to compete with such dumping prices. And, one has to add, Capitalism loves dictatorships. That's why Margaret Thatcher once expressed her admiration for Chilean fascist dictator Pinochet, and even Lech Walesa, Nobel peace prize bearer for his "Solidarnosc" movement demanded the release of the dictator who was held by an international arrest warrant by a Spanish judge seeking extradition for facing trial for the tens of thousands of disappeared. The hypocrisy is in its impertinence unprecedented when European politicians criticise Fidel Castro or Hugo Chávez for being "Stalinist" dictators. Those people who still say it after having visited Cuba or Venezuela forget that under Pinochet they would have been "6 foot under" if they only had voiced doubt about the beauty of the dictatorship. In Venezuela the worst that can happen is that one is ignored by the *Commandante*.

NEOCLASSICAL MODEL ADVANCED AS A TOOL FOR NEO-COLONIALISM

Already 33 years ago the United Nations agreed on a charter of the economic rights and obligations in which it has emphasised that any state would have the right to self determination, also and especially in regards to the choice of the economic system as well as its social, political and cultural principals in accordance with the people's will and that the use and ownership of the respective country's natural resources would be regarded as the sovereign decision of each state.

The demand of a new world economic system had been the result of different world order as the dark age of colonialism was overcome by national liberation movements in most of the former colonies. The US's defeat in the Vietnam War had also contributed to an all of a sudden much higher self esteem of the oppressed people. This was also accomplished by a new cooperation between the OPEC states which led to the oil exporting nations to claim much more of the revenue for themselves. This also inspired other countries to negotiate minimum prices for other export-products. The ruling establishment of the rich industrialised countries had understood: "The South" was to declare itself independent and by this became a threat to the economic system imposed by the former colonial powers who still made huge profits on the back of the exploited "third world". The major industrial nations conspired from now on to defend their interests. As the group of the "developing countries" gained an ever bigger influence at the United Nations, the richest and most powerful industrialised countries counter-caricatured new structures of the block-free states as well as the Group77 by founding their own organisations by this reducing the influence of the United Nations which increasingly became marginalised.

Mafia – like structures dictated through IMF and World Bank

The first G7 meeting was held in 1975 and it soon had the connotation of a meeting of a noble club. It should later develop to a club that could be seen as a Mafia connection as one of the members would help the other in a combined effort to eliminate any chances for a truly free market and fair trade. Following the first meeting of the G7 in 1975 the industrialised countries managed very well to put any attempts to create an alternative world economy to rest. A central role played the so called "Recycling of Petro Dollars" by which the revenues from the OPEC members were more or less directly handed over – through major international banks – to the elite in the 'developing countries'. The next step was to hand out cheap loans to the so called "Third

World" and by this fulfil the South's demand for an increased financial engagement without fundamentally changing anything in the financial dependence. To the contrary, the dependence of the developing countries was even deepened by these loans. In a way, the future exploitation of the South by the former colonial powers through the transfers was laid. This also led to an increased non-solidifying momentum in the so called "Third World" as some despots enjoyed the influx of capital while real progressive governments who acted in the interest of their people were confronted with bankruptcy and not seldom with violent conflicts either stirred within the respective country (like in Nicaragua, El Salvador and Colombia) or even from outside. Unforgotten is the day the US bombed Panama as they bombed away the government of the populist and relatively socialistic president Noriega who was accused of being a drug dealer, something that should not take anybody by wonder as neighbouring Colombia had their Drug Barons ready to take over the business in Panama City and build US style shopping malls and creating an offshore financial centre which would have been unthinkable under a socialistic appearing president who had put the emphasis on education and healthcare. Today's generation in Panama barely knows how to read and write. Their parents did and also had all their teeth in their mouths. In Nicaragua, with the leftist government of Daniel Ortega, a friend and follower of Fidel Castro, the US sought another direct confrontation which can be seen as more of a symbolic nature. An example had to be executed. The country was too small to have posed any threat to either the region or even the US themselves. And, the economic output of the tiny Central American country was small enough so that the people living there did not need the US – sponsored civil war sparked by Commandante Franklin's and Ernesto Cardinal's *Contra Rebels* revelation of which almost led to the impeachment of President Ronald Reagan who was able to hide behind Admiral Pointdexter and Lieutenant Oliver North. Shit happens. The so called "Third World" was split between those who "behaved well" and received loans from the rich industrialised nations and those who, because they appeared to be a more socialistic as they were listening to their people were at best sidelined and because of that less developed and in most cases also had to endure a lengthy and bloody civil war, the rich world sponsored. The loans as well as later the 'development aid' had become a very efficient tool to corrupt the elite of the so called

"Developing Countries" who opened up their markets for the US as well as the former colonial powers they had thought to have gotten rid off. Even today we can see a deviant government in Colombia to read the ALCA – free-trade – wishes from Washington's representatives lips.

HOW *SPEEDY GONZALES* GOT INTO THE TRAP[16]

Speedy Gonzales, the fastest mouse of Mexico, went into the trap when the US at the end of the seventies radically raised the interest rate. The interest payments of the "developing countries" tripled within a short time so that a further servicing of the loans was all of a sudden out of reach. The declaration of insolvency by Mexico in 1982 marked the beginning of the international debt - crisis. More and more countries, in the end 60 were counted, had to declare their bankruptcy. Most of them were African or South American countries. Instead of calling-in a conference on how to resolve the crisis the International Monetary Fund (IMF) was founded. The nature of the "restructuring programs" this institution representing the banks of the donor countries, was neo-liberal and led into disaster in most countries that had to deal with it. Poverty increased while the assets of the state were first privatised and then pledged as security with the donor banks. A sell off of the natural resources of those countries prior to taking loans would have meant for the poorest countries to have at least 15 times more of a revenue of what they got when they had to privatise and then hand over these to the rich countries banks. That's how corruption in a capitalistic society works: Bribe a tiny elite-group to take loans and when pay-back time has loomed blame them for not being efficient enough and demand "restructuring and economic reform". The next elite which so far has not taken any bribes will liquidise the rest of the country's assets and sell off the remaining resources and take those subsidies and "development aid" that has not evaporated already as an incentive for not having been bribed. The method of the system is *bribingly* easy and vice versa.

---

16   This article has already been published in the book "De-Mock-Crazy" in 2007

Strangling developing countries forcing them to starve

The problem of the ever deepening disparity between debt and annuity has not been solved and probably won't be until the last gold and diamond mine has been exploited and the last worker has taken a breath in the coal and cadmium mines in Africa. Whereas the so called "Third World" owed some 600 billion US-Dollars to the Rich World in 1980 it is today closer to 3.2 trillion US Dollars. It has not doubled or tripled, it has become five times of what it was 28 years ago without any further capital having been advanced to a viable development project. Such a return on investment, even if it is not paid back (one can write it off the tax!!!) has never been achieved by any conservative investment offered by any of the major international institutions.

Because of the mounting international pressure the G 8 summit gathering in Köln in 1999 'generously' offered a debt relief for the poorest 42 nations of some 100 billion US Dollars.

But first of all this 'debt relief' had been directly linked to a neo-liberal reform package which ridiculed any attempt to eliminate poverty in those countries. Secondly, those promises had not even been lived up to: So far only 22 of the 42 countries have experienced any debt relief while still most of the African and Latin American countries spend much more money on servicing these loans than on their budgets for education and health care.

How these "debt relieves" can soon be turned into "debt revives" has been demonstrated by the case so called "vulture funds" provide for. Because of the debt relief some countries ratings with Finch's or Standard & Poor has risen a tiny bit making them subject for collectors to take it away from them through international courts of the *Western Free World.*

Reality check: 'Chicago school' led ad absurdum

Quite a revealing article had been published by Milton Friedman in 'Essays in Positive Economics' in University of Chicago Press in 1966. It is important to have a look at this particular article of Friedman again as the entire neo-classical model of our times rests on the philosophical approach of Friedman's axiom of positive science John Neville Keynes had formulated in his book 'The Scope and Method of Political Economy'. Until today, the neo-classical economic approach follows a rather non-scientific approach of verification and falsification based on vague assumptions and predictions for which pompous mathematical constructions are developed. The trick applied is very simple: make the mathematics employed that complicated that only mathematicians understand it while keeping the underlying assumptions and predictions that vague and global that their falsifications are virtually impossible and then say that what one couldn't *falsify* has to be regarded as *verified*. In a nutshell this is the method Milton Friedman and his followers of the 'Chicago School of Economics' have applied over the decades. They and the political elite of the capitalistic world used these tools to discredit any alternative economical model although their own model neglects theory but favours ideology in a way as one could say Charles Darwin served Humanism by advocating the survival of the fittest credo.

The Chicago School of Economics advanced in the 20th century to *the* promoter of the neo-classical model which we see today once more crash and destroy wealth, standard of living of the majority of citizens on this planet and ultimately life on Earth.

In his article of some 40 years ago Milton Friedman writes that "the conclusion of positive economics seem to be, and are, immediately relevant to important normative problems, to questions of what ought to be done and how any given goal can be attained." By this, he admits that conclusions do have political relevance although he had always maintained that the Chicago School was exercising science and not politics. By creating a kind of a scientific body like a 'school' the neo-classicists could very well hide behind a presumed 'scientific neutrality' which made it easier for politicians to refer to them when pushing through the profit maximization interests of the rich class. It is because of the latter that the article of Milton Friedman becomes so relevant today. Over half a century the financial capitalism tried to brainwash the global population with semi – scientific but highly mathematical propaganda in order to justify ruthless social cuts and a distribution of income and wealth that has now being led ad absurdum as it created overcapacities on one side and under-supply on the other, by creating poverty despite a continuously rising productivity and over-indebtedness although per capita we all steadily become richer than ever before.

Friedman and his followers always made sure that all their theories appeared to be tautologies and in a way self-evident, but that, of course is easy if one can set the axioms right so that it just suits. He writes: "Positive economics is in principle independent of any particular ethical position or normative judgements. As Keynes says, it deals with 'what is' not with 'what ought to be'. It's task is to provide a system of generalizations that can be used to make correct predictions about the consequences of any change in circumstances. It's performance is to be judged by the precision, scope, and conformity with experience of the predictions it yields. In short, positive economics is, or can be, and 'objective' science, in precisely the same sense as any of the physical sciences." Here one can study how manipulative the neoclassic ideologists operate. They pretend to be neutral but they don't construct an economic model that adequately describes the reality but create tautologies based on irrelevant or unpractical assumptions which' sole purpose is to manifest an income and wealth distribution that cements a world order in which the rich become richer and the poor poorer.

A bit later Friedman writes that "Proponent (of minimum wage) believe / predict that legal minimum wages diminish poverty by raising the wages of those receiving less than the minimum wage as well as of some receiving more than the minimum wage without any counterbalancing increase in the number of people entirely unemployed or employed less advantageous than they otherwise would be. Opponents believe/ predict that legal minimum wages increase poverty by increasing the number of people who are employed or less advantageously and that this more offsets any favourable effect on the wages of those who remain employed." Here, Friedman like all of his followers until today do it, takes the rise in productivity completely out of the equation. He doesn't take into account that the technological development requires less labour and in most cases less energy in producing a good and that because of that one could easily say that a wage increase is affordable because of the rise in productivity. Especially when he wrote that article the technological development was at times revolutionary and automatisation as well as later computerisation had made many inefficient manual and labour intensive productions superfluous and replaced these by machines. Instead of setting the predictions of the equations of the neoclassical model in a fair way of sharing the additional wealth created by workers, inventors, entrepreneurs and investors Friedman and his 'school' until today maintain that the rise in productivity almost exclusively benefits the owners and shareholders of the enterprise but not the workers. Logic, Friedman and the Chicago School of Economics were not in business with the underprivileged but the ruling class.

Just another, tiny, little bit later, Friedman reveals what he really thinks about unions and government involvement: "Closely related differences in positive analysis underlie divergent views about the appropriate role and place of trade-unions and the desirability of direct price and wage controls and of tariffs. Different predictions about the importance of so called 'economies of scale' account very largely for divergent views about the desirability of necessity of detailed government regulation of industry and even of socialism rather than private enterprise." His position is clear: any government involvement is counterproductive.

Friedman rather suggests to build a hypothetical construction of assumptions and predictions which have to be falsified or verified by a reality-check. But, in his own models he allowed only the prediction to be the base to determine whether the assumption is right or wrong, a classical tautology which only works within the system. What if the prediction is wrong? It is that absurd that one could, following Friedman's method, for instance proof that Earth is flat. All one needed is some supplementary assumptions or rather auxiliary assumptions which are easily construed as we know from the sparring between Nicolaus Copernicus and the Vatican. Friedman and the Chicago School of Economics could for instance, according to their own method, say that the assumption that the eclipse of the moon was artificially generated by an external light from behind heaven.

In reality, Friedman's 'Chicago school' and their followers have created almost-impossible-to-solve mathematical constructs like the 'Euler equation' which usually consist of variables that result from assumptions and predictions which are hard to establish in the real world or can not be measured and therefore make it impossible to falsify the theory. One could, for instance assume that economic decisions of people depends on the colour of their eyes. By this assumption one could maybe proof a theory. The tragedy with Friedman's attitude is in fact that the Chicago School of Economics as well as many others that followed love to develop such completely useless models and that an entire economic model has been created from it. Following Friedman the so called 'Real Business Cycle Theory' had been developed on the same principles Friedman so openly laid in front of us in his article of 1966. Said theory predicts that the economy goes up and down because of the technology shocks but in the end reaches equilibrium again. In Micro economics this may be true, but this theory for instance suggests that when productivity rises the labour demand decreases because, the theory goes, people re-define the optimum of their work and spare time relation. In other words, because people live better, they work less. That's why the unemployment rate is increasing, the theory wants to tell us. Everyone who sees the queues outside the recruitment agencies will be able to falsify this theory without any question. But, on this kind of theory the neo-classicists base their macro economical models.

Friedman writes that "viewed as a body of substantive hypotheses, theory is to be judged by its predictive power of the class of phenomena which it is intended to 'explain'. Only Factual evidence can show whether it is it is 'right' or 'wrong', or better, tentatively 'accepted' as valid or 'rejected'. (…) the only relevant test of the validity of a hypothesis is comparison of its predictions with experience."

Friedman makes it clear that it would be absurd to criticise this theory on the ground that the assumptions are not subject to scrutiny and that the mere suggestion that the assumptions were unrealistic. One should rather only verify or falsify the predictions by the reality check. Thus he can set whatever variable and proof whatever might be in the interest of certain people and construe an equation that is supposed to 'scientifically' *prove* what he and his followers say the reality is. By this rather unscientific method one can make it look as if it was scientifically proven that everyone can become a millionaire if only he saved long enough a good portion of his income and lead a modest life and after 40 years or so inevitably become a millionaire. This legend is being told again and again and many people believe it, but somehow the wealth of 4/5th of Americans stagnated or declined over the past 30 years while the income and wealth of the top ten per cent of society exploded.

THATCHER DE-INDUSTRIALISED GREAT-BRITAIN AND LOOK WHERE THEY ENDED RELYING ON *THE CITY*

Also, the recovery of stock markets in the summer of 2009 which many official analysts who are these days completely Friedman-infected say is the silver line at the horizon indicating that the end of the crisis is near is anything but the real economy getting back on track. Logic, that some of the massive funds pumped into the system by President Barack Obama and Timothy Geithner and the European government's 'stimulus packages' eventually trickles down to the consumer but this is rather marginal. What does indeed happen is that with all the freshly printed money new bubbles are fuelled. One can, of course, continue with bubble building even into perpetuity, as long as someone buys the trash papers being issued and re-issued but what remains left over can be witnessed in the UK: a de-industrialised country that relies on the dubious snowball business of *The City* by which Lady Thatcher had replaced coal and steel industry. Adam Smith would not have liked that, Karl Marx would have laughed about her.

Any empire whose elite had thought they had invented a system to become and stay rich without working degenerated and painfully declined until it was extinct by evolution.

The sudden hype about rising steel prices that many analysts cite as being proof for economic recovery again was totally unjustified as it entirely rested on the Chinese suddenly increasing demand. In theory, especially in Friedman's theory, this would mean that China produces more goods again and for that reason needs more steel. But, the reality is different from theory again. China has, by building up trillions of US Dollar reserves, only one interest: not to let the American economy crash completely as this would devalue their assets. In China there is a lot of speculative money circulating these days and this is responsible for the 'steel bubble' as we will most likely call it when it bursts. Worldwide the steel prices are rising as everyone hears about the suddenly increased

Chinese demand. In Russia, the steel industry celebrated a 12% growth in July 2009 compared with June 2009, even Japan increased it's steel export by 17%, most of it to China. But, what does China do with all that steel? Mainstream economists these days explain to us that an economy of more than 1.2 billion people who are trembling with their feet waiting to be allowed to consume since Western life-style has been introduced to China are responsible for the increased demand. That's bullocks. China lives solely on export. To use the imported steel for domestic consumption would be crazy as one would have to change the Dollar reserves for that which would immediately slump the Dollar dramatically – a film the Chinese certainly wouldn't want to watch. No, the truth is that the Chinese state-capitalistic elite has learnt from the West how to build bubbles and to become rich by snowball systems just too well.

ACCORDING TO NEO-CLASSICAL MODEL ALL THE BUBBLES WOULDN'T EXIST

Generally, one could ask whether it is possible that GDP rises while domestic demand declines. In theory, it would be possible, even indefinitely, but it wouldn't be healthy. Mainstream economists who try to tell us that all will be fine and the world economy be back on track, soon, are interpreting figures like follows: in period one, let's say the first quarter of a year, 100 cars are being sold, 5 of which from a previous production, so only 95 cars have to be newly manufactured. That is the real GDP. In the following period, the second quarter, again 100 cars are being sold with now only 2 stemming from the previous period (1), so in order to be able to sell 100 cars one has to manufacture 98 anew. The GDP grows by three cars from 95 to 98 or by stunning 13.2% on an annual basis although in reality the same amount of cars are being sold. Even if the demand for cars in the following, third quarter of the same year is declining from 100 to 98, the annual GDP growth would still be measured as 4.3% although less cars are being sold. This way it is possible to show growth rates when there is actually a slow down or even decline. Insane, but that's how the Friedman's of our world construe their economic models they manage to sell for half a century now to all of us. It is the basis of the bubble-economy that strangles the real economy.

According to the neoclassical model all these bubbles wouldn't exist. Milton Friedman, if he was still around would probably explain this by changing the parameters of his science once more and introduce assumptions and predictions into his mathematics in order to make it suit again. He and his 'school' would argue that the crisis only happened because of too much state and not because the financial markets were left to supervise themselves which we have seen is equivalent to letting monkeys mind a banana plant. Friedman probably would have, like many of the usual suspects of the neo-liberal analysts nowadays do it, argued that the liberalisation and deregulation has not been far reaching enough and that this is why our economies got into crisis, in other words only because we weren't effective and fast enough in demolishing social systems, privatising health care, education and pension schemes and not ruthless enough in demanding every living person to justify her or his existence. It would have been likely that he had interpreted the sudden recovery of the stock markets as an indicator that the system can be revived by shock therapy, but one should rather not look at where the liquidity for the patient's transfusions are coming from, as one would discover that they came from outside the system and not from within which actually proves that the neo-classical model simply doesn't work. In Friedman's world one should send away the emergency doctors from the patient.

POLITICAL LEADERS INFECTED BY FRIEDMAN'S IDEOLOGY

How much our political leadership is infected by Friedman's ideology becomes evident when one scrutinises the way EU Commission and national governments are fighting the crisis they call 'credit crunch'.

The EU Commission is increasing the pressure on the Romanian government to exercise strict fiscal austerity, reform the pension system (rather privatise it) and cut down on public expenditure, in other words all the usual neo-liberal tools that will have drastic effects on the standard of living for the majority of citizens. In a country like

Romania one can imagine what the economic decline will be like: under-supply in basic needs and maybe starvation.

The IMF and EU Commission made it clear that the times where Romania was welcomed as a new member by financial presents (which only reached the corrupt elite in Bucharest anyway) are over:

"Reflecting lower growth, public revenues in 2009 are also lower than expected by about 3.5% of GDP" the EU Commission announced on 10th August 2009 saying that "the government agrees to additional spending cuts of about 0.8% of GDP in 2009 in order to contain the deterioration in the budgetary situation. Structural reforms will also be stepped-up to continue the budgetary consolidation beyond 2009."

There can not be any doubt what is on: "This will include further measures to restructure public sector employment and to strengthen fiscal discipline in local governments, decentralized entities and state-owned enterprises. This is on top of the implementation of a Fiscal Responsibility Law, currently under way, and reforms of the public wage and pension systems" said the EU Commission spokesperson.

"Real GDP contracted by 6.2% year on year in the first quarter, more than expected when the Romanian economic adjustment programme was agreed in June, as a result of worse-than-expected domestic demand and external environment. The authorities' new growth projections for this year have been downgraded to around -8/-8½% from -4% previously with only a modest recovery expected in 2010, as weak household financial conditions and rising unemployment will keep domestic demand low" the EU Commission reiterated. Will they let Romanians starve after they so peacefully had surrendered their industries on a silver plate to Western European multinationals?

EU INSTITUTIONS AND NATIONAL GOVERNMENTS LET LOBBYISTS WRITE THE LAWS

At that time German Economics minister Karl Theodor zu Guttenberg, in Chancellor Merkel's new cabinet Defense minister, doesn't even dare to outsource his ministry's formulating of a law on how to deal with troubled banks. Mr. zu Guttenberg who is poised to become youngest ever Chancellor of Germany one day asked the international law firm Linklaters to formulate the new law which will effectively help banks evade nationalisation in case they get into trouble and require state aid to survive. Instead of having his own ministry hammer out the details of such insolvency law he asked said law firm which in it's day to day operations handles bank insolvency cases amounts to asking frogs lay dry a moor. It is clear that Mr. zu Guttenberg doesn't trust his own ministry and it's 1,800 officials to come up with a 'feasible scenario' which allows banks to be rescued by taxpayer's money without actually be put under effective control by the state. The minister's proposed law will be seen as the last resort for banks and make it extremely comfortable for the bank's owners only to have to endure some control by the state but not being asked to surrender their shares in exchange for state aid. It would rather be in the interest of the Federal German government and the German taxpayer that the money that is spent on bailing out or for rescuing troubled banks resulted Euro by Euro in ownership rights of the public. But, at times when the EU Commission is choosing a bias approach when it comes to state aid being granted to private banks one could certainly not expect the German government to be more 'liberal' in the traditional meaning of the term and simply let the democratically elected officials take care of formulating the rules and regulations under which state aid is granted.

The EU Commission still pursues infringement proceedings against Germany for a 5 billion Euros bailout of state-owned WESTLB, a classical Landesbank, owned by public Sparkassen, while letting the German government get away with it's 485 billion Euros bailout-guarantee - package for mostly private banks in Germany. If one asks our political leaders why they take this clearly bias approach towards favouring private banks they don't even deny it but argue exactly along the lines of Friedman and the Chicago School of Economics according to who any state intervention is seen as interference and that the market will sort it out by itself. They do forget, of course, to mention that the only one, who can foot that bill, is the taxpayer.

It is shocking to see who and for what is awarded a Noble prize of economics. Respectable scientists like Stiglitz and Krugman should consider returning theirs.

NOT A THEORY, JUST BLANK IDEOLOGY

The Chicago school of economics which had so lustfully introduced neo-liberalism by their elite economists such as Milton Friedman who loved to be on photos with Pinochet, and Cavallo in Latin America which in many countries led to dictatorships and fascist regimes like in Chile and Argentina, is led ad absurdum. It is time to show the advocates of such economic theory that it is not only anti-economical but from a scientific standpoint nonsense while under humanitarian aspects it is nothing else but barbarism. It can be seen as quite cynical under this aspect that the beneficiaries of such brutal regimes, major corporations like Ford and others generously donated through their foundations money to human right organizations, also Amnesty International, and other respected organizations under the condition that only the tools of dictatorships and fascism are branded but not the economic theory that actually stood behind it. It's a shame that capitalism loves dictatorships or it is simply logic. As when the people are imprisoned, at least the prices can be free.

FROM FRIEDMAN & PINOCHET TO SACHS, THATCHER, WALESA, YELTSIN, MENEM & MBEKI

Milton Friedman's ideology and his epigones at the Chicago School of Economics indeed had transformed the world in a way one could only describe as revolutionary although it rather was *counter-revolutionary* since it came without any philosophy or culture but the only doctrine that is best described by the 'survival of fittest' – credo which under humanitarian aspects can only be seen as barbaric. My dear colleague Naomi Klein calls the Friedman-strategy *Shock Doctrine* and is certainly right with that as she gives a detailed account of the shocking truth about the human toll or in Bush's terminology the *collateral damage* of our economic system.

Wall Street got nervous when Salvador Allende became the democratically elected President of Chile in 1970 and started socialistic reforms that were also shining over the borders across all of Latin America. The Chilean copper mines which until then had been owned by a US company were to be nationalised. The American mining company had over 50 years invested a billion Dollars in the copper mines but transferred some 7.5 billion Dollars each year home to the US. When in 1973 Allende's party won additional seats in the parliamentary elections it became clear that Chile would for a long time be rather a socialist country than anything the American industries could arrange with. It were economists educated by Friedman and the 'Chicago school' that plotted together with CIA and Chilean military against President Allende and install a junta under General Pinochet. Catholic Church and the Chicago school had conspired a long time before 1973 and sent students over to Chicago to be infiltrated by Friedman's ideology. The *Chicago Boys* took over key positions in the regime that killed tens of thousands of people and led to a mass exodus from Chile. The economic strategy of privatisations, deregulation and social cuts has been in it's entirety adopted from Friedman's *Capitalism and Freedom* which rather bluntly described the neo-liberal tools that were now mixed with the torture tools of a military regime. Colleague Naomi Klein neglects a bit the theoretic background for such ideology but she perfectly describes what the consequences have been. The first 18 months Pinochet followed exactly the Chicago-rules and privatised many but not all state owned companies among them several banks. The latter were then allowed to engage in snowball system like financial speculations. Pinochet also opened the Chilean market and invited imports which ruined Chilean producers. Government expenditure was cut back by 10%, price control laws which had over decades kept basic needs free from inflation. Following these radical reforms inflation skyrocketed in 1974 to 376% especially for basic subsistence goods such as bread. At the same time mass unemployment cost hundreds of thousands of Chileans their social existence because the domestic manufacturers couldn't compete with the imports. The *Chicago Boys* argued that not their theory was the problem but that it has not been stringently enough been applied. They demanded further social cuts and more privatisations. The sole beneficiaries of this economic strategy were foreign companies and a group of financiers, the so called 'Piranhas' who made a fortune by speculations, but not the traditional industries that initially had supported the coup d'état against President Allende. In March 1975 Milton Friedman and another leading economist of the

Chicago School, Arnold Harberger, followed the invitation of a major bank and flew to Santiago de Chile in order to rescue the experiment. Chile's mainstream media celebrated Friedman as the guru of the new order. And, Friedman himself lauded the extremely wise decisions of the dictator but pressed Pinochet to cut social expenditure by at least 25% over the next six months. Pinochet replied that the plan was in full swing and fired his economics minister and replaced him with an even more radical 'Chicago Boy', Sergio de Castro. Government expenditure was cut in 1975 by another 27%, mostly in health care and education. The public school system was replaced by chartered schools for which one needed vouchers, writes Naomi Klein. Healthcare was reformed in a way that one had to pay in cash for medical services but the most radical reform has been the privatisation of the Chilean social security system. Economics minister de Castro privatised some 500 state-owned companies and banks of which most were given away as such bargains that one could say Santa Claus appeared twice in that year. In addition to that many more trade barriers were knocked down resulting in an immediate loss of 177,000 jobs leaving the share of producing companies in total GDP to be marginal. In the first year of Friedman's shock-therapy the Chilean economy shrank by 15% and unemployment jumped up to 20% whereas it had been below 3% under President Allende. Average Chilean workers and employees had to spend 74% of their income on basic needs such as bread whereas it had been 17% they had to spend for bread, milk and public transport under President Allende. Many of the Chicago school- economists personally inspected the Chilean experiment, even Friedrich von Hayek, a man often brought into connection with the European Fascism, visited the country several times. He had been kind of a guru for Milton Friedman.

In 1982 the Chilean economy collapsed under exploding debt, hyperinflation and 30% unemployment. One of the reasons for the sudden collapse has been the fact that the total deregulation dictated by the *Chicago Boys* and Pinochet allowed the 'Piranhas' to create a debt bubble by buying up any of the state's assets by borrowed money. In the end they accumulated 14 billion Dollars in debt.

Only because of the disastrous situation the dictator was forced to deviate from the *Chicago Boys'* concept and nationalise many of the companies, a bit like our governments do it these days with the banking sector. The *Chicago-Boys* as well as de Castro lost their government offices. Ironically, the sole reason for the state not to collapse completely under these conditions has been that Pinochet never privatised Codelco, the Chilean national copper mines that President Allende had nationalised. This company generated 85% of the country's export income. That's why the state still had some income when the *Chicago Boys'* bubbles burst. In 1988, when the Chilean economy finally regained some stability, the country was impoverished with 45% of the population living under the poverty line. At the same time the income of the top ten per cent of society had risen by 83%. Until today, Chile is one of the countries accounting for the biggest gulf between rich and poor.

It is quite remarkable, that until today, the American establishment's preference so openly is made visible by such little things like the *Microsoft* text-programmes' spelling check: Pinochet is known by the dictionary of *Microsoft* XP but Allende isn't.

The economic minister of long time Argentinean president Carlos Menem, Domingo Cavallo, one of the most outspoken advocates of Latin American Neo-Liberalism and a follower of Friedman's Chicago school of Economics is still pulling the strings behind the scene in an effort to counter-caricature President Cristina Fernandez de Kirchner's attempts to re-nationalise pension schemes and undo other privatizations of the Menem-Cavallo years.

PRESIDENT RAUL ALFONSIN FEARED THE *CHICAGO BOYS* LIKE THE JUNTA

The late president Raul Alfonsin who had been the first democratically elected president after the junta had lost the Falkland war and stepped down leaving an enormous debt that laid the seed for the next crisis had been toppled by Menem and Cavallo who in economic terms rehabilitated the junta and their beneficiaries by reversing the economic course of solidifying finances by privatizations and liberalizations. A scandal, given the fact that Cavallo was already serving the junta that let thousands of people disappear. It was him who dictated all privatizations in Argentina. The IMF and World Bank only copied what he had written beforehand. Then, it was sold to the Argentinean public as the dictate of the IMF. Still, the *Chicago Boys of Latin America* are held in high esteem in certain circles. When I interviewed former President Raul Alfonsin in 2003, twenty years after he had assumed the presidency[17], he admitted that he had wished he could have done better but was held back by the mere fact that he did not have the budget to finance the social programs due to the heavy debt of some 65 billion Dollars that the Junta had left behind. When I asked the old president why he had not tried what Presidents Eduardo Duhalde and Nestor Kirchner did and re-negotiate the foreign debt he responded that he had considered it but knew that if he had done that, that the junta would have come back.

In a way, late President Alfonsin can be seen as a tragic hero: he did what he could but the people of Argentina could never see it clearly as the neo – liberalism of Menem and Cavallo had carried the long shadows of the Junta had only vanished when they voted right-wing. And, Raul Alfonsin was able to bring Junta Generals into court or the Truth Commission to investigate the crimes, but if he had touched the upper class' method of income and wealth distribution he had gone too far and he was keenly aware of that. Even today, it is not certain that Argentina will be spared from falling back into a police-state or even a military regime but as long as the Argentinean people vote for semi-democratic right wing parties like during the June 2009 parliamentary elections, this danger can be excluded. But, President Cristina Fernandez de Kirchner has to be careful. She took over the bankrupt pension funds and re-nationalized the system saying it was in the interest of the workers. But, suspicion goes around that fiscal need may have been a bigger motive[18]. As the soy beans price had fallen dramatically the fiscal income from external trade can not make up for the wage increases in the public sector Mr. Kirchner had pushed through before the presidential elections in 2007. So far, the Kirchners managed to appear a bit more leftist but if the government is not trusted anymore and a real leftist force would come into play, one could fear that the military came back as well. When I interviewed at that time President Eduardo Duhalde in April 2003 he told me that "the power of a president in this country was quite limited."[19]

---

17 Watch the interview at www.ralphtniemeyer.com
18 The Economist 23rd October 2008
19 "The White Train" documentary film Argentina 2003

But, although the juntas had been wiped away the Chicago-strategy continued as the democratically elected governments had taken over the debts accumulated by the military regimes. Argentina had debts of 7.9 billion Dollars before the coup d'état but when the junta had lost the Falkland war and was replaced by the democratic government of President Raul Alfonsin, it had been 45 billion Dollars of debts he had to deal with. Argentina became subject to blackmailing by major banks, the World Bank, later the IMF. Small Uruguay had half a billion Dollars debts before the junta took over but after it was ten times more: 5 billion Dollars. In Brazil it was even more drastic: 3 billion Dollars before the military stole the power and in 1985 when the generals had finished the democratic government inherited 103 billion Dollars in debts which laid the ground for the debt crisis in the 1990ies. Most of the debts had been used up by military and police commanders and brought abroad. Just before the dictatorship ended in Argentina, the Central Bank president Domingo Cavallo who became economics minister under Carlos Menem and is still seen by many in the Argentinean upper class as a genius declared that the state would take over all these obligations and guarantee the debts of domestic as well as multinational companies which like the Chilean 'Piranhas' had accumulated incredible debts. Beneficiaries of this generous act were Ford, Chase Manhattan, Citibank, IBM, Mercedes Benz and others.

Citing the necessity to consolidate the state finances President Carlos Menem and Domingo Cavallo who had both conspired against President Raul Alfonsin since he had taken the oath of office as the first democratically elected president after the dictatorship, privatised and sold almost everything the Argentine state ever owned, mostly to Citibank, Suez, Vivendi, Repsol and Telefonica. Naomi Klein finds proof for the Argentinean 'shock-program' to be written by the country's largest creditors, JP Morgan and Citibank. More than 1,400 pages dictated to the Argentinean government in great detail how to privatise public subsistence, how to reform employment laws, pension system and any of the state's assets. Menem and Cavallo followed that plan by an almost Prussian accuracy and with the verve of the Sicilian mafia. Until today, the Argentine mobile phone system is the most inefficient and expensive system on the entire American continent. Nowhere else would it be possible to charge customers for incoming calls and also have a domestic roaming system. On top of that the service falls back well behind mobile phone services of other Latin America nations of which the majority is considered to be developing countries. Just recently the Argentinean President, Cristina Fernandez de Kirchner, re-nationalised the pension system but her motivation was only partly driven by the idea to rescue the savings of future generations. It has rather to do with the fact that she aims at bridging the state's budget deficit. The Peronists have not fully departed from Cavallo's legacy yet.

From Chile to Argentina, Russia and South Africa the same symptoms are to be noticed: a speculative maniac bubble created in major cities of a region or country promises huge returns and mega profits sidelines everyone who came too late to participate. But, these bubbles are based on dubious expertise by 'analysts', brokers and 'investment' bankers who are hardly able to understand any of the underlying 'theories' of Friedman & Co. The 'boom' is accompanied by a hype and hectic consumption in the middle of ghost-industries and rotten infrastructures which represent a past development from which half of the population is excluded. Corruption and nepotism usually get out of control, small and medium sized entrepreneurs are downsized amid a massive transfer of wealth from public into private hands which is followed by an equally massive transfer of debt from private into public hands. Similar developments like in Chile had been observed in other Latin American countries, too: Brazil had been governed by a US-backed junta which let several of Friedman's former students avail of government positions in the late sixties. Milton Friedman travelled to Brazil at the height of the kill & torture regime in 1973 and declared the Brazilian economic experiment to be a miracle. In 1973 the 'miracle' was expanded towards Uruguay and in 1976 the government of Isabel Peron got toppled by the *Chicago Boys* and landowners who had organised themselves in the *Sociedad Rural* and who at the same time were occupying positions in various major multinational corporations. Price controls fell which let meat prices jump up to 700%. Opening of the Argentinean market as well as the abolishment of any hinder for foreign companies to buy shares in Argentinean companies along with a privatisation – wave resulted in disaster. Wages lost 40% of their value within a year's time while industries shut down and poverty spread. More than half of the population fell under the poverty line. More than 30,000 persons 'disappeared' during the years of the junta. Chile, Argentina, Uruguay and Brazil had become the laboratory of the Chicago School of Economics and Friedman's doctrine.

Meanwhile, international banks pleased the torture regimes with cheap loans and credit-lines. But, there has been a distinct interdependence: It would not have been possible to implement the Chicago-doctrine in democracies and the dictatorships would not have survived without the banks operating under Chicago-rules. Especially the unions in these countries had become the target of the juntas and their death-squads.

Naomi Klein proves that attacks on unionists had been conducted by employers such as Ford Motor Company and Mercedes Benz. Several of these multinational companies employed private death and torture squads like in Brazil. Just ten years before the people in Southern America had enjoyed booming industrial sectors and better education and health care and had been looked at like a model for developing nations, but suddenly rich and poor were economically separated. "The people were imprisoned so that the prices could be free", the Uruguayan writer Eduardo Galeano said and it seems that we are heading towards that road again. Three weeks after the former minister in the Allende government, Orlando Letelier, got assassinated in Washington D.C. on 21st September 1976, Milton Friedman was awarded the Nobel Economics prize for his work on the interdependence of inflation and unemployment. Friedman's hypothesis for which he had received the Nobel prize was led ad absurdum by the masses of hungry Chileans who queued for bread, suffered under typhus and mass unemployment.

At this stage it is important to shed some light on the various human rights organisations such as Amnesty International (AI) and others who branded the brutal torture regimes but failed to mention the connection to the Chicago school and Friedman's ideology as well as the economic interests major multinationals had pursued by dealing with these regimes. Colleague Naomi Klein cites the 1976 Amnesty International report on Argentina which she says fails to mention any of the junta's economic decrees that lowered wages and increased prices. Also, no other but the military structures were blamed by AI for torture and killings although CIA, multinational corporations and domestic landowners were directly involved as well. Said reluctance of human rights activists to mention the economic factor of the dictatorships certainly has to do with the fact that these organizations are awash with money donated by exactly those corporations or affiliated foundations that are aligned with the juntas, such as the Ford Foundation who in the 1970ies and 1980ies financed the Chilean Peace committee and American Watch and others by some 30 million Dollars. Same Ford Foundation earlier had financed the scholarships for Chilean students at the University of Chicago and by this created those brutal rulers of Latin America. It only can be seen as symbolic that it had been Ford cars in which people were abducted by the fascists.

Admirers of Friedman and Pinochet in Europe tried their best to adopt the Chicago school's doctrine but were facing some resistance and hurdles which under normal circumstances could not easily be implemented in democracies. British Prime Minister Margaret Thatcher needed the Falkland war in 1982 to re-instate her popularity which had been diminished. But, having carried home a clear victory she took up the fight against the powerful coal worker's union in 1984 which she managed that well that she also broke the resistance of less powerful and less influential unions. Then, the iron lady privatised British Telecom, British Gas, British Airways, British Airport Authority, British Steel and also sold the government's shares in British Petroleum, in other words, the entire country's silver cutlery. No private owner had been that stupid to give up his most profitable long-term investments and that all the aforementioned state owned corporations had been bargains for those who bought it is evident as otherwise there wouldn't have been any buyers. Clear that Lady Thatcher who had told Pinochet many times that she admired what he was doing defended him when the former dictator was arrested in London upon an international arrest warrant by a Spanish judge. But also Lech Walesa, another Nobel laureate and ex president of Poland, jumped at the side of Pinochet. Maybe it was only logic as both seemed to have shared a particular anti-humanistic ideology. Likewise did the Polish Pope John Paul II never criticise Pinochet and when he visited Chile had no time to meet with the Mothers of the Disappeared.

Generally, the political climate at the beginning of the 1980ies had changed with the juntas collapsing under huge debts. Wall Street and the owners of industries and banks, the High Net-Worth Individuals (HNWIs) and Ultra-High Net-Worth Individuals (UHNWIs) as Merrily Lynch calls them, certainly had reason to become nervous as authoritarian regimes were wiped away by revolutions and up-risings, be it like in Iran where the Shah was overthrown and replaced by a clerical regime that nationalised the banks, re-distributed land and controlled import and export. Or, in Nicaragua where the Sandinistas of Daniel Ortega took the power after a people's uprising against the Sumoza-regime.

Another important player in the big game Friedman and his 'Chicago Boys' played has been George Soros, the infamous speculator who later brought down the European Exchange Rate Mechanism (ERM) and the British Pound in September 1992 by speculating against it so that it fell by more than what the agreed leverage had been. Prior to that Mr. Soros got involved in the collapsing Socialist Eastern European sphere by sending over his 'henchmen', Jeffrey Sachs and David Lipton, a free-market fetishist of the International Monetary Fund (IMF), as 'advisors' to Lech Walesa's *Solidarnosc*. The plan of the three had been more radical than in Latin America. The government under Nobel Peace Prize bearer Walesa abolished any price control laws, cut state subsidies and privatised any and all of the state's assets, from coal mines, shipyards to industries and state owned company despite *Solidarnosc's* initial promise to have these being democratically administrated. In addition to that Mr. Sachs helped the Polish government to negotiate a deal with the IMF under which Poland was granted a one billion debt relief in exchange for a ruthless liberalisation and deregulation strategy while subscribing to fiscal austerity that resulted in a decline of industrial production by more than 30% within 2 years letting unemployment hit the ceiling. In 1989 15% of the Polish population had lived below the poverty line but in 2003 it were already 59% with a further upward trend since joining the European Union.

USSR GIVEN AWAY FOR AN APPLE AND AN EGG

Other examples for the strategy of Milton Friedman, George Soros and Jeffery Sachs are easy to detect when one studies the history of the Eastern European socialism and the decline of the Soviet Union. I interviewed President Mikhail S. Gorbachev[20] shortly before the Soviet Union ceased to exist and he told me how disappointed he was that the Western Free World which had thanked him enthusiastically just a year before for introducing *Perestroika* and *Glasnost* along with ending the Cold War and opening the Berlin Wall, then dropped him and supported Boris Yeltsin who opened the Russian market and surrendered all the industries without any resistance. Gorbachev admitted that he had not expected that at all and had hoped to be able to do the transition slowly and well-coordinated but he had miscalculated how quickly former Communists transformed into capitalistic oligarchs and collaborators with Western banks who de-industrialised the entire Soviet Union and put Western European products onto the shelves. IMF and World Bank did the rest which led into disaster in 1998 when a severe financial crisis destroyed the wealth and savings of millions of Russians. Today, the number of alcoholics as well as unemployed has doubled compared to Soviet times. More than 50 million children live below the poverty line in the Ex Soviet Union countries as UNICEF reported.

A DE-INDUSTRIALISATION WAVE SWEPT THROUGH RUSSIA

When one travels by train or car through Russia these days one sees many derelict industrial sites which all have been operational during Soviet Union times. They may not have been as efficient and as productive as Western European or North American companies but they gave their employees work and they produced something and not only stood around like industrial monuments. But, the logic of the free market and capital amortisation the Chicago School of Economics dictates to despots and world leaders is a one-way-street only: it only

---

20   Extracts of the interview are available at www.ralphtniemeyer.com "No peace. Never."

wants others to open their markets and allow foreign capital to amortise in such market at any cost, be it social rights, environmental principles or the social existence of millions of people that are sacrificed. The only difference between the US and Western Europe in case of the Soviet Union is that in addition to imposing our financial system onto Eastern European countries we also gave them our top-shelf products. The Americans didn't bother about that too much as they didn't produce much anyway. What strikes me is the fact that Mr. Gorbachev as such a brilliant politician and highly intelligent man as he is had been so naïve that he could not see what should have been the obvious: that the West had only one interest: opening market and imposing it's profit maximization rules.

THE WEST'S UNDERSTANDING OF 'DEMOCRACY': BOMB THE PARLIAMENT!

That it was easier for the West to pursue this strategy with a drunkard who killed his last brain cells by every vodka bottle he emptied when dancing to the tune of the western leaders and bankers had been another issue a man like Mr. Gorbachev should not have been surprised about. When I met Mr. Gorbachev again in June 2008 in the European Parliament[21], almost twenty years later, he said to me that indeed, he was very concerned about the course Russia has taken and that he felt sorry for his country and that he could not manage better to keep people like Yeltsin at bay. Even the parliament at that time that had resisted Yeltsin has then been shot at in November 1993 by Yeltsin and the new elite of the country, namely those oligarchs who first stole the rest of the industries and then even bought football clubs in England, Mr. Gorbachev told me. The unbelievable idea of many Eastern Europeans who dreamed of democracy that the Soviet Union and Warsaw Pact would be rescued by the West shows a great deal of naïve thinking. The reasons for West Germany having been granted a Marshall plan after WWII have been first of all the fact that the US wanted to dominate Europe, open markets and find strategic partners in a developing cold war and secondly, simply because the Soviet Union and an alternative economic system did exist. Without Eastern European Socialism, no

---

21   Watch the press conference here: www.eureporter.co.uk

Marshall plan and no *social* free market – cushioned Capitalism had come into existence in West Germany ever. The reasons why a Lech Walesa had been supported by the West has been the same why 'Gorbi' has been loved by us: he promised to surrender Polish interests on the altar of the *Zeitgeist* which unfortunately has been a neo-liberal one. That's why both Nobel peace prize bearers are political outcasts in their respective countries but still loved in the West.

If Russians had studied the case of Poland they could imagine what it would be like if Capitalism of the kind of Friedman had been introduced to their country. USSR president Mikhail S. Gorbachev was blackmailed by the G7 in 1991 that in case he wouldn't agree to a radical economic shock therapy they would let him down. In fact, the Soviet Union was dissolved on 25th December 1991. I had spoken with Mr. Gorbachev just days before and he told me that he was very disappointed by the western leaders who had first lauded him for introducing democracy and freedom of speech but then suddenly supported a man like Boris Yeltsin. The day when Yeltsin took over from Gorbachev, I saw that Jeffrey Sachs was in the Kremlin, too. I witnessed how he explained to Yeltsin that if Moscow agreed to introduce Capitalism in Russia, that some 15 billion Dollars could be granted as aid from Western banks and the IMF. Part of the deal has been the abolishment of price controls, budget cuts and rapid privatisations. Yeltsin agreed, shot at the parliament where there was still a lot of resistance and gave away industries and banks to friends and family members. The new rich class of oligarchs who controlled the key industrial sectors of Russia opened their companies for multinational 'blue-chip' companies who secured themselves a huge piece of the pie. In 1998 the Russian economy collapsed completely and a year later Yeltsin got replaced by Vladimir Putin who still privatises industries but also restores centralised power – pretty much to his St. Petersburg circle of friend's advantage.

The catastrophe couldn't have been worse and the former KGB circles around Mr. Putin who had their own economic interests feared that the situation could get out of hand as consumption had declined within only one year from 1991 until 1992 by 40% as more than a third of the Russian population fell below the poverty line. In 1998 more than 80% of Russian farms were ruined and about 70,000 state owned companies were shut down which led to mass unemployment. Whereas it had been 2 million people who lived below the poverty line (less than 4 Dollars per day) in 1989, ten years later it were 74 million Russians. Alcohol consumption had doubled since 1989 and today, also the suicide rate. When I spoke with former President Mikhail S. Gorbachev again in June 2008 he admitted that he was very sad about the development and had wished to have had the power at the particular time to have averted the course, history had taken. Well, what can one say? Maybe that we all influence history by what we undertake to do as well as by what we refrain from doing.

MANDELA DIDN'T SERVE 28 YEARS TO SEE THATCHERISM

Another good example for the success of the doctrine advocated by the Chicago School of Economics is South Africa. I had followed the first free elections in South Africa[22] and followed both main candidates, ANC president Nelson Mandela and President F W de Klerk and spoken with both of them. At that time a wave of violence swept through South Africa as there has been disagreement between various black tribes and especially between the Inkatha Freedom Party of Kwa Zulu Natal - King Zwelethini and Prime Minister Buthelezi and the African National Congress of Nelson Mandela. The focus of the world in that election has been on Nelson Mandela winning the political power but what had happened beforehand behind the scenes has been a sell-off of South Africa. That was one of the reasons for the disagreement between black tribes. The ANC once had promised to return the mines to the people of South Africa by nationalising diamond and gold mines but while all eyes were focused on the human rights issue, one seemed to have forgotten that there was an economic issue as well.

The South African whites have been extremely clever in out-manoeuvring the blacks by granting them equal rights, voting rights and even handing over political power to them while having comfortably negotiated that the South African central bank remained independent, the mines which generated such a great return for a few white families

---

22 Extract of the documentary film are available at www.ralphtniemeyer. com/documentaries/ballade-of-the-stone

and other private property remain untouched. The leading figure in those negotiations with the white government has been Thabo Mbeki, the only one in the ANC who understood a bit about economics and had learnt in his exile years in England what a good idea Thatcherism was. He guaranteed the whites that they wouldn't loose out when the ANC would take over.

When Mr. Mbeki followed Nelson Mandela as president in 1999, he applied a tough neo-liberal economic agenda that led to privatisation of water and electricity and other public subsistence. Former President Nelson Mandela had probably asked himself many times why he had not insisted on stirring the economic course as well, but the answer could have been that he had never been released from prison and the country might have sunk into a never ending civil war. Since the ANC took over government in 1994 the people living under inhumane conditions and from less than one Dollar a day has doubled. Criminality is at a peak. Back then, in April 1994 I had asked both, ANC president Nelson Mandela as well as President F W de Klerk whether they didn't fear that after abolishing Apartheid officially a social Apartheid would pose a danger. Both said that, indeed, the feared that this could happen. But, they also both cited that there was no alternative to their course and that other economic solutions had failed. That was true for their times. Socialism had collapsed only five years before in Eastern Europe, so it was not the right time to speak about Marx and nationalisations when the rest of the world danced to the tune of Friedman. Not only because of that is it right to say that Nelson Mandela has been released much too late from the white man's jail. He had also been needed to stay longer in power to make Mbeki impossible as his successor.

In January 1990 Nelson Mandela wrote from his prison compound to his followers that "the nationalisation of the mines, banks and monopoly industries is the policy of the ANC, and the change or modification of our views in this regard is inconceivable. Black economic empowerment is a goal we fully support and encourage, but in our situation state control of certain sectors of the economy is unavoidable." The African National Congress's (ANC) freedom charter dated 1955 had made it crystal clear what the goal was: right to work, decent housing, freedom of thought, national wealth be restored to the people. "The mineral wealth beneath the soil, the banks and monopoly industry shall be transferred to the ownership of the people as a whole, all other industry and trade shall be controlled to assist the well-being of the people" the ANC freedom charter states. Indeed, Apartheid had been not only a political but also an economic system, like Fascism also hasn't been solely based on racism and chauvinism but exploitation. In South Africa Apartheid had been a highly lucrative system of maintaining a class system allowing a tiny, white, elite to draw all profits from mines, farms and industries. As Naomi Klein points out the negotiations over brining Apartheid to an end were held on two parallel tracks. On one track, which we journalists of the Western Free Media, me included, had exclusively been focussing on, had been the political negotiations between Nelson Mandela and F W de Klerk, while in the meantime Thabo Mbeki negotiated the economic agenda between ANC and National Party (NP). I do remember well that all the press bulletins always mentioned human rights aspects but not any major point about the economy. When I asked President F W de Klerk about it he very vaguely said that the task groups were dealing with that and find a consensus in all those questions as well. And, when I spoke with ANC President Nelson Mandela during the election campaign an advisor interrupted me when asking about the economic parameters that had been negotiated between the ANC and NP. I was told that Mr. Mandela had only agreed to be interviewed about the elction campaign. So we spoke about Soweto and Kwa Zulu Natal instead.

The ANC had agreed to the White's demand for keeping the central bank independent and also to leave Chris Stals and Derek Keyes in their positions as central bank president and finance minister. Moreover, Mbeki agreed on behalf of the ANC to have a passage be written into the constitution that would protect all private ownerships by this out-ruling a land reform or any nationalisations. Also currency exchange controls were excluded because just immediately before the elections an 850 million Dollars agreement had been signed with the IMF which called for wage moderation that excluded any rises in minimum wages. The ANC also had signed GATT making state subsidies for car and textile manufacturing impossible. In June 1996 Thabo Mbeki introduced a neo-liberal agenda that called for more privatisations, budget cuts and labour-flexibility, less trade barriers and less currency controls. Mbeki sold the state's assets in order to pay back the debts of the white oppressors.

Since 1990 the situation of the black majority has worsened. The general life expectancy has declined by 13% while the amount of people who have to live on less than 1 Dollar per day has doubled and now is above 4 million people. The unemployment of black citizens has doubled as well and is around 50% nowadays. And, although the ANC government had built 1.8 million houses more than 2 million had lost their homes. Also, whereas 9 million citizens had been connected to water supply 10 million have been cut off by the private water company because the prices were unaffordable. 50% more people (25% of the population) nowadays live in sheds in slums without clean water and mostly without electricity. Nelson Mandela had been washing his successor's head many times but Thabo Mbeki continued with his neo-liberal politics until the end of 2008.

CHICAGO BOYS RUINED LATIN AMERICA, EASTERN EUROPE & AFRICA

As long as we let the principles of the Chicago School of Economics and people like Milton Friedman and Jeffrey Sachs rule over this planet, there will only be suffering and no real free society ever will develop.

I won't go more into detail about the actual fall out of our present economic system as my colleague Naomi Klein had brilliantly and in great detail given account on what she described as 'Shock Doctrine'. My only aim is to complement her research by giving the background of the economic theory that indeed is the real cause of the symptoms she described perfectly. Many activists seem to believe that the present crisis is a result from individual greed of ultra rich and major corporations but that criticism as justified as it is falls short of laying bare the givens of a mathematically incoherent economic theory, to which the greed by individuals is only having an enhancing effect. The problem is deeper rooted: the present economic system is not based on theory that stands up any scientific scrutiny but only ideology. It is an ideology that can also be described as the "survival of the fittest".

Just one little side-note on Iran:

AHMADINEJAD RULES BY MEANS OF DEATH PENALTY AGAINST LEFTISTS

In case of Iran, German corporations are said to have threatened it's Iranian employees to lay them off if they took part in the anti-government protest that had followed President Ahmadinejad's re-election. *Knauf Gips KG* wrote on 21st July 2009 to it's employees in it's Iran based Knauf Iran, Knauf Gatch and Iran Gatch, that the "employees were not only representing their private opinion but also the company" if they became "politically active".[23] What a contradiction! Usually, Western Free World corporations dislike Ahmadinejad because he still doesn't open up his market and keeps it under Iranian control, but somehow he obviously stands for a certain stability in the country. Since the Iranian Revolution thirty years ago a lot of things have changed in the country. It has become more open and liberal, in some way even neo-liberal axing social rights Ayatollah Khomeini once had introduced although these were combined with a clerical impetus. But, since a few years the country has undergone some rather neo-liberal changes that clerical leaders who also control the business had approved and by this are selling off piece by piece the Iranian Revolution. Meanwhile, President Ahmadinejad keeps leftists at bay by the means of the death penalty and that is of course in the interest of companies, especially foreign companies. What the US Americans don't like about Ahmadinejad is that he was not doing his neo-liberal reforms fast enough and did not open up the Iranian market, that's all.

THE MECHANISM OF THE METHODOLOGICAL INSANITY

A few words on the mechanism employed by the hedge fund junkies and bankers who all must have lost their heads by completely ignoring any risk assessment rules a good banker would adhere to:

The trillion-fold wealth created by said mechanism is strangling our economies today. In principle, the mechanism has been less complicated

---

23   Spiegel online 01st August 2009

than most people would think. Let's say a millionaire, Harry, who either inherited a million or won the lottery or robbed a bank, wishes to multiply his million. Thus he invests it in the investment fund "Rich Fast Track" which borrows another 100,000 € from his bank in order to enhance the potential profit maximization. For the now 1.1 million Euros he purchases stock, let's say from Chrysler. Now, a second millionaire, Dick, comes into the equation. He also invests a million Euros. He gives it to another investment fund, called "Skyrocketing Profit" which borrows 200,000 € on top of it from his bank because the investment fund managers like to spin a bigger wheel but also have a greater risk exposure. The "Skyrocketing Profit Investment Fund" buys the Chrysler shares from the "Rich Fast Track Investment Fund" for 1.2 million Euros. Thus they have made 100,000 € profit of which they pay out half of it to their investor. The other half the clever investment fund managers of "Rich Fast Track" use to cover their bank's interest and pay themselves some nice bonuses. Harry is now very happy, too as his investment made a return of 50,000 € in a very short time. He re-invests his 5% return immediately, so "Rich Fast Track" now administrates 1.05 million Euros of their client Harry. And, because everything went so extremely well, the investment managers now take out a loan of 300,000 Euros from their bank and buy Chrysler shares for 1.35 million Euros. Probably those which they had sold to "Skyrocketing profit Investment Fund" earlier on for 1.2 million Euros. "Skyrocketing Profit" has indeed lived up to it's slogan and made a speculative profit of 150,000 € of which they pay their investor Dick 50,000 € and use the remaining 100,000 € to cover their banking costs and keep their managers happy with a nice bonus. Also Dick has received a nice return of 5% which he immediately re-invests with "Skyrocketing Investment Fund" which in addition to the 1.05 million Euros they have from their investor Dick take out a loan of 450,000 € from their bank and buys the same Chrysler shares from "Rich Fast Track Investment Fund" for 1.5 million Euros. The "Rich Fast Track Investment Fund" now accounts for a nice net profit of 250,000 € of which 150,000 € are paid out to millionaire Harry who by now has made 200,000 € in profits and doesn't see any reason for terminating this beautiful game, so he re-invests his 1.2 million Euros and "Rich Fast Track" now decides to spin an even bigger wheel by borrowing another 1.2 million Euros from their bank. The Chrysler shares are now being bought for 2.4 million Euros leaving "Skyrocketing Profit" with a phenomenal profit of 900,000 € of which they pay millionaire Dick 600,000 while they put the remainder into their own pockets and pay their bank the interest for the previous transaction. This game can continue in perpetuity as long as either new investments are coming in or ever higher loans are granted by which they finance the ever higher prices they pay for the Chrysler shares. It is obvious that the entire process of these transactions economically is nonsense. Nothing is being produced, no new technology invented, not a single car more being sold but the share prices of the car manufacturer Chrysler is going up each time a new transaction is closed. Nevertheless, new income has been generated, new 'wealth' created, but not produced. In total 1.4 million Euros that not only statistically count as new income have been generated with the 200,000 € of return on investment for Harry and the 650,000 € for Dick but also the bonuses for the managers of the investment funds "Rich Fast Track" and "Skyrocketing Profit" and their bank's interest. Neither macro-economically nor for society as a whole have these gains any positive effect, but on the other hand very negative ones as Dick and Harry, but also their investment fund managers want to enjoy their newly created wealth although they haven't worked for it. But, in most cases, this new wealth is not spent on higher consumption or on the goods market but is rather used to generate more money. One can certainly question the legitimacy of such insane virtual reality wealth accumulation, especially when taking into account that such artificially generated liquidity is used by every Dick and Harry to execute ownership rights over existing industries and demand as *owners* an ever higher return or higher profit rates and when these are not possible to achieve by increasing production or by innovating the product and by this increasing the sales figures, by eventually cutting down on wages, social expenditure or even by pulling their capital out for the sake of more profit to be made on the financial markets leaving the manufacturing industry without liquidity to refinance it's production and forcing it into liquidation despite a previous profitable production. That's exactly what has happened in the wake of the financial crisis which for that reason has spread like cancer into every single corner of the real economy.

The volume of the artificially created liquidity which are directed by ultra-rich individuals and their financial institutions, the sophisticated and almost impenetrable mostly offshore jungle of companies, their almost unlimited credit potential explain our present financial system's instability and it's addiction to excesses and exaggerations.

The crisis of the financial system is not a problem because it endangers the wealth of the rich, but because a stabile financial system with banks who grant credit lines to the real economy is vital for our economy. But, the financial institutions of our days did the opposite of financing production, innovation and inventions. It simply made speculators richer and richer. And, not only does it sound quite impertinent that those Dicks and Harrys who are now fearing to lose their financial playground and possibility to make money without working demand to be bailed out by the general public, but the financial capitalistic system is also fundamentally anti-economical by creating a tremendous pressure on companies to lower wages, cut investments into innovation and inventions in order to increase the shareholder value. And, it is anti-humanistic as our political leaders are sacrificing our standard of living, our health care and pension systems, public subsistence, schools, libraries, universities, theatres and concert halls over bailing out every Dick and Harry who had made and lost a fortune by useless speculations.

WOODEN PLANKS LAID OVER THE MORASS

Since the insolvency virus had brought proud investment houses and banks down to their knees, mainstream economists, bankers and politicians call for regulation and even nationalisation. As we seem to be heading for a directed economy it could be worthwhile to point out the methodological flaws.

For some time, the banking sector may be stabilised by the state interventions.

But, without fundamental reforms which ought to include the Sword of Damocles in form of the liquidity bomb created by Hedge Funds and Private Equity Firms there won't be any cure in sight.

As much as the measurements taken by the EU summit of 16th October 2008 should be welcomed it also should be noted that the underlying problem of our present economic system is *not* the credit crunch.

It rather is the constant struggle between profit-rate, balance of production output and demand. It doesn't help to fight the symptoms (liquidity crisis) but not the cause (production-demand imbalance).

Unless this struggle is dealt with properly, a solution to the present crisis is impossible.

Our leader's attempts to dry out a moor by laying branches of trees and ever more planks on top of each other may for a while let the path we are walking on appear to be safe.

But, it is not a very clever way of dealing with the struggle our economies since a long time are fundamentally confronted with.

DEMAND-CURVE VERSUS INVESTMENT-DYNAMIC

An economic model in which the demand defines the expansion of production that is solely limited by technological possibilities is sustainable. The capitalistic production in which the consumption is limited by production output once more collapses.

Unfortunate for the neo-classical model is that capitalistic production is limited by the necessity to allow the invested capital and it's accumulation to create a certain profit rate or so called 'return-on-investment'. The shareholders want to be fed.

The crux of the present crisis is buried in the fact that the deadly foam of the financial markets feeds itself from reservoirs of an economic system which only produces and invests if the return on investment for the capital owner is enticing enough and which degrades wages, social contributions and corporate taxes to cost factors that need to be reduced.

The priority is profit, not demand.

This is the reason for instability and crisis that even a regulated capitalism always creates. The more successful companies can reduce such 'costs' the more difficult it becomes for the entire economy to sell newly produced cars, mobile phones and flat screen TV sets.

Purchasing power is not only defined by the absence of inflation but also by the level of wages which ideally should keep pace with the increase of productivity. The cat is biting itself in its own tail no matter how cheap the production has become. Without positive sales figures there is no profit and without profit there is no return on investment.

On the other hand, profit rate and wages can simultaneously rise if the productivity of labour increases, but the purchasing power from wages never can contribute to the profit share. It always remains a cost factor in relation to the return on investment.

THE INEVITABLE CRASH IS BUILT INTO THE SYSTEM

That's the trouble with Keynesianism. It only works for a limited time, like the infusions by governments into the ailing financial system.

Necessary investments are not being made. Important tasks not been taken on. People laid off although there is enough work around.

The most important components of domestic demand which define the standard of living of the vast majority of people in a society are in a capitalistic economy always merely a side-product. That is because profit margins are streaming out of the arteries of financial speculation, not investment, production and consumption.

In an economy which' life elixir solely is drawn from profit rate and return on investment it comes along as a logic conclusion that those artificial wells are to be kept liquid by whatever means. Those can be credit-financed speculation and upper-class consumption. We have witnessed that this results in financial bubbles being created that stand in no relation to the real economy's production output and rise in productivity.

A credit-financed purchasing power and domestic demand - be it by the state or the consumers' banks - is limited by an inevitable over-indebtedness even though these limits can be pushed towards the edge for quite some time as we have seen in the US.

But, all the solutions within the frame of our present system rest on economic imbalances which sooner or later would have to become even if the system shall be sustainable. The later this is achieved the bigger will be the crash and no political leader will wish to be blamed for it. The latter may explain why our leaders so desperately try to keep the rotten banking system alive as anything else would mean to let the entire system drown in the morass of an unsustainable economic model.

Like in 1989 when the (so far) last version of directed economies expired by imploding none of our leaders seems to be brave enough to draw the right consequences and avert an explosion.

A THIRD WAY?

Almost twenty years after the Soviet-style socialism collapsed world-leaders prone nationalisation and regulation while vowing to shut down tax havens, hedge funds and private equity firms. It appears as if Capitalism didn't win over Socialism but only outlasted it. Is what is coming now really new, maybe offering the chance to finally go the Third Way, Socialists in France, Social Democrats in Germany and *New Labour* in Great-Britain had dreamed of or is it rather a pragmatic approach that lets Marxism sneak through the backdoor in the hall of mainstream politics?

In a, under humanitarian aspects, barbaric but undoubtedly growth and productivity enhancing way capitalism in its early days swivelled from upswing to crisis, back and forth. Back then it has been mostly the investment dynamism which produced an upswing which led to an increased employment, greater profit rates, ever more consumption and just before the boom peaked to higher wages. Just, when the ever more enhanced capacities created by such a prosperous economy started to produce as well, it became clear that it were too many so that the willingness to invest got slowed down which resulted in an even greater lead of supply over demand. At this point, back then, as it is today, prices started to fall. This let the purchasing power of the wages go through the roof while profit share rapidly declined bringing any investment cycle to an end.

Socialism gave us a lot, after it took it from us. Capitalism gave us a lot, but it didn't leave anything behind.

V.

SOMEONE *MADE-OFF*

How stole the raisins from the pie?

While the public as well as private debts exploded during the past three decades there can also be an incredible multiplication of accumulated wealth noticed. Like on a balance sheet of a company there is a 'minus' on one side and a 'plus' on the other. But, one could hardly operate a company successfully if the debts are exploding and are kept on the balance sheet while at the same time the profits are hidden from the shareholders by parking them in an offshore account without appearing on the balance sheet. Literally speaking, this is what the planet's elite has been doing with us. In 1970 the entire wealth bubble accounted for 12 trillion Dollars but until 2005 it has been 12 times of that figure, more than 140 trillion. The world GDP was totally decoupled from the wealth explosion and while developing countries in the so called "third world" had to starve their populations to death in order to make room for yet another bubble that followed each and every privatisation and opening of the various markets, the workers, employees and SMEs in the industrialized countries were given credit cards instead of wage increases and over-priced mortgages and expensive loans in order to finance consumption and production. Although some of the accumulated wealth also vanished each time when one of the smaller or even bigger bubbles burst, there has been no such crash (yet) that interrupted the constant growth of the financial wealth. On the contrary: financial wealth grew ever faster and now amounts to ridiculous four times of the World's GDP meaning that if all these owners of the virtual funds all of a sudden wanted to withdraw their money and buy goods, such as designer clothes, furniture, high-tech and whatever valuable, it would not be there in sufficient volume. A dramatic devaluation would kick in. In other words: the worldwide financial wealth market is kept alive by dodgy cheques.

But, what makes piles of virtual money so attractive is not the hypothetical possibility to consume such excessive wealth but rather the fact that it guarantees it's owners further income without forcing them to work at all. Dividends, interests and capital gains since the 1970ies have experienced a steep increase in it's share of GDP in all OECD countries. This increase has been the result as well as the cause of the exploding monetary wealth. Result because greater wealth results in bigger income and cause because the vast majority of such income is not consumed but re-invested.

This self-enhancing effect allowed the owners of big capital to concentrate more and more economic power in their hands. Even though this concentration may only be nominal and couldn't be realized the entire mechanism does have a tremendous impact on the real economy. The increases in stock and share prices and ever higher payouts create immense pressure for the management to at least keep the level of the payouts at whatever costs otherwise the share prices may drop. The sword of Damocles of a capital withdrawal is hanging over each and every management decision. That's why redundancies are becoming an option even in economic good times. If the only way the level of payouts can be maintained is by cutting down on labour- and production costs, the management will go for such even though it is a one-time effect and even though it may damage the company's future performance because of such cuts. Many companies which had profitable operations had reduced staff and were winding down business if less than 8% profit were made over a year. This results in a vicious cycle in which the management is forced to put aside ever more capital for the shareholders in order to keep the return on investment high enough to attract further capital which again is not invested in any sensible way but to a large degree dedicated to pleasing the shareholders in the next round. A dreadful disparity between shareholder income and production growth is becoming a gulf.

In the end these huge amounts of virtual funds are increasing the power and influence of the financial industry, the banks, hedge funds and investment funds which direct decisions in the real economy as well as in our societies of which the recent rescue missions for the ailing financial house of cards by our political leaders is a clear proof. Billions and soon trillions of taxpayer's money are dumped on the graveyard of the bubbles the owners of big capital created over decades who still profit from the debts we all have to shoulder and for which we are told to tighten our belts.

So is it true that we all simply had to save a little bit more money in order to be on the sunny side of life? Well, the most important predicament for a happy saving are high incomes. But, the average citizen will never be able to save enough money in order to be allowed into the millionaire's and billionaire's clubs. In all countries at all times the saving's rate grows in line with increasing income. Extraordinary high incomes are achieved in our present economic system by those who do not work but let others work for them. That's the reason why only a marginal portion of the world's wealth results from savings made from work-income. The vast majority of the real big capital results from inheritances and re-investment of already existing wealth. A study on capital wealth in the US concludes that 80% of the total American financial wealth results from inheritances[24]. That's probably not different in Europe. The fact that big capital creates big income and by this poses as a self-enhancing model is the reason why financial wealth is even less equally distributed than income. Below is an overview of the distribution of financial wealth in the various income percentiles in the US between 1998 and 2001.

---

24 Kotlikoff, L. J., Summers, L. H., The Role of Intergenerational Transfers in Aggregate Capital Accumulation, (Journal of political economy, 1981, vol. 89, no. 4)

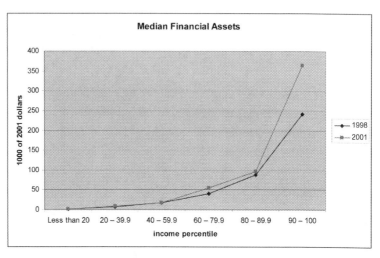

Median Financial Assets

SCF 2001; gross wealth of all families with income

The two curves indicate the over-proportional concentration of wealth at the top 10 % as well as the over-proportional growth of wealth of the richest group of society in the years between 1998 and 2001. Interesting is the fact that the bursting of the dotcom bubble obviously not only didn't harm the rich class but even benefited them while small and medium investors who had been led into the market too late lost most of their assets in the Clinton-Gore internet-hype.

In OECD countries wealth generally is concentrated in a few hands. More than 50% of families in industrialized countries do not account for any wealth at all while the richest 1% own and control more than half of all financial wealth. These are the people the broker house Merrill Lynch in his *World Wealth Report* refers to as 'High Net Worth Individuals (HNWI) and who own more than a million Dollars in cash. In Germany for instance there were just 800,000 persons who had a million Euros on cash deposits. According to Merrill Lynch there were 10 million HNWIs worldwide in 2007 who owned all together some 40.7 billion Dollars, half of all privately held cash deposits.

In industrialized countries typically the HNWIs are the top 1% of society. By this, one can say, wealth today is much stronger concentrated than in 1929 which for a long time has been referred to as the most perverse wealth concentration. 80 years ago, 1 % of the richest in the US had owned 40% of the total cash deposits.

These millionaires and multi-millionaires for who every bank roles out the red carpet are also the main beneficiaries of any hype, be it driven by stocks and shares or obligations. In Germany 70% of all privately held stocks are owned by the top 1% of society. Only 8% of the German population own stocks, so in a way it is a funny thought that the rest of us, the 92%, have to listen to the news reporting from the DAX-, Nikkei-, Dow Jones- and NASDAQ – 'Casinos' every day. In the US the stocks held in private hands is about 20% but the concentration is equally insane. Within the HNWI – group there is another even more exclusive club: the so called Ultra High Net Worth Individuals (UHNWIs) who by definition account for more than 30 million Dollars in cash deposits. At present there are 100,000 UHNWIs globally and they can be seen as the global monetary aristocracy and main beneficiaries of today's financial capitalism. They were able to let their income and wealth explode over the past 30 years as they profited more than anybody else from the privatizations, profit maximizations and bubble buildings. The head of the global wealth management of JP Morgan Private Bank said that these UHNWIs account for 30-40% of all financial assets.[25]

Generally, one can conclude from all statistics that the bigger the portfolio, the greater is the growth in that sector. The income and wealth of the UHNWIs grow much quicker than any other household's portfolio. Whereas the HNWIs saw their global wealth grow by 9.4% in 2007, the UHNWIs could witness their wealth explode by 14.5%.

But, even within the UHNWI-group of the ultra rich there are still distinctions been made: the Crème de la Crème of the global monetary aristocracy are 1,000 billionaires which are listed by the Forbes Magazine. These billionaires are topping the UHNWI wealth explosion by skyrocketing 35% annually like in 2007, the year in which the present worldwide crisis had it's beginning on 11th August. Interesting, that in contrast to the public finances which got into severe trouble by the financial turmoil of August 2007 the wealth of the richest did not suffer at all from the crisis it has caused by it's excesses.

---

25   Financial Times 07th July 2004

The fact that wealth grows the faster the bigger it is has been proven by the Forbes data in 1995-1998. The wealth of the richest 400 Americans had grown by 95% from 379 billion Dollars to 740 billion Dollars clear of inflation within those three years. But, even that have been peanuts in comparison to the wealth explosion of the richest 10 multi-billionaires who could multiply their wealth by 270%.[26]

One can also see in the real economy who benefits from the financial capitalism: stagnation and recession of mass products are countered by an ever greater prosperity of the luxury goods sector. In 2006 alone 159 billion dollars of luxury goods were sold, 9% more than in 2005 and 50% more than in 2000. In the last three months of 2007 Richemont, a typical provider for luxury goods who recruits his clients from the UHNWI list, increased his turnover by 14% although the financial crisis had just begun and the British bank Northern Rock had experienced a bank-run by it's smaller clients.

The hunger of the ultra rich to maximize their profit requires an ever more ruthless re-distribution of wealth. The so called Gini coefficient which reflects the income distribution and by this indicates the disparity between lower and higher incomes has risen since the early 1980ies dramatically, especially in the Western industrialized nations[27].

The following graphic shows explicitly who benefited from the development of the past 20 years:

---

26 Arthur B. Cernickel, An Examination of Changes in the Distribution of Wealth. From 1989 to 1998: Evidence from the Survey of Consumer Finances, 2000

27 Galbraith, J.K., Kum, H., Estimating the Inequality of Hs. Incomes: A Statistical Approach to the Creation of a Dense and Consistent Global Data Set; Review of Income and Wealth, Series 51, Number 1, March 2005

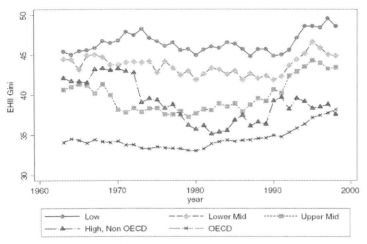

Source: Galbraith, Kum (2005)

It is, of course, totally irrelevant for the standard of living of an UHNWI whether his wealth grows by 2, 5 or 20% per annum or whether it stagnates. He or she will always be able to shop at Richemont and only use a marginal amount of his money for purchasing goods of the real economy. Nevertheless will said Ultra-High-Net-Worth-Individual always make sure that his money be multiplied by the best possible investment which his bankers, hedge fund managers and brokers may find. In the centre of the financial capitalism has been the task to maximize the profit for the richest families and to make those richer who own already more than they themselves, their children, grandchildren and great grandchildren can consume in the next one hundred years to come. Tools in this bizarre game of such insane profit maximization are wage dumping, social cuts, tax avoidance schemes, redundancies, closing down of profitable production sites, reduced investments, neglected innovations and minimized research, but also economic and military blackmailing of entire countries and wars of aggression including occupation of sovereign nations, dictatorships and torture regimes.

The result of this wealth and income distribution are slowing down productivity and growth figures, a declining standard of living for billions of people, destroyed economic capacity, social injustices and growing poverty. The present system is a methodological insanity that results from the logic of an …economic system which sole driving force is the creation of private profit. During certain periods and under specific conditions this driving force has contributed to making the economy more productive and society in it's entirety richer, even though said richness has always been distributed unequally. Today's financial capitalism instead has replaced the creative and productive destruction in Schumpeter's[28] understanding by the destruction of creativity, productivity and wealth.

HOLY COWS THAT DON'T GIVE MILK ANYMORE

Why the US' decline affects us all:

The US managed to let their growth and productivity statistics shine as if it was the biblical star above Bethlehem. International investors, banks and sovereign wealth funds sent billions over Atlantic and Pacific and were given trash-paper in exchange for that.

There has been a lot of talk about the "booming 1990ies" in the US. Not only, defenders of Clinton and Gore maintain, have there been dotcom-bubbles but also real investment. Truth be told there was no such thing as any significant real economic growth.

The trick employed by the Clinton-Gore administration had been the hedonic pricing which due to quality adjustments allow improved goods be recorded as economic growth although only the consumption expenditure rose but not the number of sold cars, electronic goods and houses.

Problem with hedonic pricing is that although quality improvements increase the standard of living these can not be measured or quantified. But, on paper it looks good to say that consumption has increased by 5% even though this was only because of price increases.

By this method one can also eliminate inflation while the real economy's growth appears to be stunning. This led many people to believe the legend of a new technology investment-boom in the 1990ies. The figures showed a five times higher investment in that sector than

---

28   Joseph Schumpeter, Austrian economist

10 years earlier. But, if one scrutinises the nominal figure it shrinks to less than half of it.

The boom in the new technology sector solely stems from an increased quality standard of processors as well as software which have been fictitiously been added to the real investment expenditure.

Without hedonic price-clearance the investments made in manufacturing industries let all those marvelous growth figures of the 1990ies look rather modest. However, the faked investment dynamics the US showed to the rest of the world and making everyone believe it was 1.5 times higher than in real terms it has been attracted huge foreign investment.

The American 'consumption boom' of the past 15 years also stems from the book of the fairies. Long lasting capital goods such as electronics, household items and furniture have not been purchased excessively as the Bureau of Economic Analysis (BEA) in Washington tries to make people believe.

According to the official BEA macro statistic the real expenditure for capital goods has between 1990 and 2004 exploded by the factor 2.5 which would be a phenomenal annual growth rate of 17%!

To suggest that the upper quintile of American society had doubled its consumption every year is hard to believe. On the other hand, wages for the vast majority of Americans stagnated and even fell drastically for the bottom 20%, so where should all this magnificent demand come from?

The truth is that the nominal expenditure of the Americans in the same time period has merely doubled. But, to assume that cars, DVD players or refrigerators were not subject to price increases in the US would be naïve.

If we look at the official consumer price index a modest annual increase of 3.5% remains from the celebrated "boom" of the Clinton-Gore – years.

And, also the much admired growth of productivity of more than 4% per annum in the second half of the 1990ies is owed to the creative accounting of the US government.

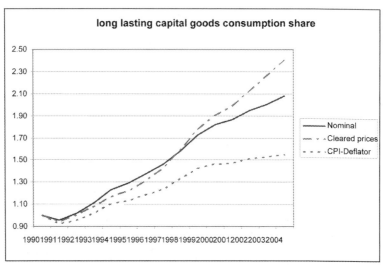

Source of data used for graphic: National Income & Product Account (NIPA)

The only miracle Clinton and Gore were able to create was to attract by such manipulated economic data foreign investment which by building bubbles financed the ever growing current account deficit of the US economy.

Latest capriole of the hedonic pricing fetishists has been the announcement that the US economy grew in the second quarter of 2008 by unbelievable 3.3% while the rest of the world already took bracing position for a sharp recession. Sole purpose of this news was to keep the show on the road. German car makers, for instance, trusted the American data and are now surprised to see the demand for Porsche, Mercedes, BMW and Audi automobiles decline by double digit figures.

The American stock markets closed positive, stocks and shares of American as well as international exporters suddenly could notice increased demand again. Not for long, though. It transpired that the US economy was hit by record unemployment, a sharp (-11%) decline in the housing sector and the collapse of the car industry which recorded a decline by 25%.

It would be time for a heart-to-heart talk between the international community and the new US administration. Those manipulations ought to be banned. And, EU Commission and member-state governments have to abide by this, too as the virtual economy's holy cows won't give milk anymore.

ANOTHER PR - STUNT BY 'SARKO'

Reporting from Paris, 04th October 2008

A sense of urgency lay over the scene at the Élysée Palace in Paris on Saturday, 4th October 2008, when at 16:45 all members of the European G8, Prime Minister Gordon Brown, Chancellor Angela Merkel, Minister-president Silvio Berlusconi as well as 'Euro-Group' chairman Jean-Claude Juncker, European Central Bank (ECB) President Jean-Claude Trichet and the president of the EU Commission, Jose Manuel Barroso, arrived in the Élysée Palace to debate measurements to be taken in the wake of the most severe financial crisis of our times.

One thing has already become clear as bail-outs weigh heavy on government's budget forcing to increase public debt: The Maastricht criteria obliging member-states to execute fiscal austerity and reduce government debt can be seen as dead right now.

Member-state governments are increasingly sidelining EU institutions as they bail-out financial institutions and banks in their various countries in defiance of EU regulations that ban state aid which has not been approved by the EU Commission.

It appears that mechanisms put in place in order to handle a crisis on EU level are ending as a paper-tiger.

At the same time the German government being confronted with further bank bail-outs in the next few days costing an estimated 200 billion Euros shows little willingness to pay into any kind of European solidarity fund ostensibly brought into play by the French government ahead of the meetings.

As this met fierce resistance of the German government the French president rowed back saying that this was not the official position of the French government. The finance minister of France, Christine Lagard, quickly said it was her private opinion she had voiced.

The German chancellor, Angela Merkel, said upon her arrival that it was "a difficult situation and that for this reason the politicians should take responsibility, but also those who caused the damage would have to contribute."

Although this sounded very different from the position reported as the one the French EU presidency was seeking, President Nicolas Sarkozy agreed with the German chancellor saying that "one only had to translate what Angela Merkel just said into French to have his position".

The German government seemed to have taken the lead as it was Mrs Merkel who said that one "will also talk about forms of prevention so that in future this won't happen again". This was also not quite what the Italian government had wished for it.

Italy's Minister-president Silvio Berlusconi had also requested a common approach as 5 major banks in Italy are facing collapse. This is especially tragic as these banks were created by privatisation of public and cooperative banks which resulted in high costs for running current accounts as well as these conglomerates dominating the financial market and fuelling the bubbles built in Europe.

As the EU Commission still pursues the infringement proceedings against Germany over the relative small WEST LB case (5 billion Euros) the German government may feel little desire to become the major contributor to a potential pan-European bail out plan. The lukewarm declaration that came out of the meeting in the Élysée Palace provides for no clear measurements but can rather be seen as a publicity stunt.

One thing has transpired, though: the Maastricht accord has silently been buried as the leaders, Mrs. Merkel, especially, said that the rules shall be applied with a certain flexibility to suit the situation.

It is clear that other than that nothing fundamentally will change as these leaders who had no real mandate to negotiate anything only agreed on a paper which said they would leave it to the various institutions to sort it out and that member states can unilaterally decide on bail-outs of banks in their jurisdiction but that at the same time no harm should be caused to other member states. This was a clear signal that the Irish government's flat-rate guarantee of six major banks was not to be approved as it leads to a de-flux of capital from other states to Ireland.

I asked at the press conference[29] how many more banks one should watch to crash before the trading of financial instruments which obviously did so much harm to the real economy were either limited to casinos or simply be banned completely.

Italian Minister-president Silvio Berlusconi replied that he wouldn't mind to have the business being transferred to casinos, while the chairman of the 'Euro Group', Luxembourg's Prime Minister Jean-Claude Juncker, said that he wouldn't want to be forced to drive by a casino to get some cash.

Mr. Berlusconi's reaction has to be seen in the light of the previous government he presided over which forced Italy's public banks to become private and by this being forced to participate in the unhealthy financial bubble building.

THE END OF EUROPEAN SOLIDARITY

Reporting from Strasbourg

EU Commission's proposed 130 billion Euros package to jump-start economy is rejected outright by Germany. Everyone, it seems, is looking after themselves during the crisis.

German industries (export-leaning) are in sharp decline.

The huge discussion about the future of Opel AG, General Motor's German car manufacturer has swept into the European Parliament in Strasbourg today as several German MEPs criticised the EU Commission for proposing a 130 billion Euros economic support program. EU Industry commissioner Günther Verheugen suggested that 1% of each country's GDP would be put behind the package the EU Commission is trying to put in place in a combined effort to jump-start the ailing European economy. But, this idea is not very popular in Germany.

---

29   The press conference can be watched here: http://ec.europa.eu/sttreamebs/
      cgi/ebs.pl?p=72894&s=128330&key=E158AC0516D4B9606717A604
      E485B1E226728547

Germany's economy unlike those of other European member states is almost entirely relying on export – most of it to the US. This week a discussion swept through Germany whether Opel, owned by troublesome GM, would be rescued by state guarantees. Advisors to Chancellor Angela Merkel said that one would have to make sure that the guarantees wouldn't be drawn by the owner, General Motors, making the German taxpayer's money end up in the pockets of shareholders in the US.

On top of that, ARD, first German TV channel, revealed that Opel AG apparently was not directly owned by General Motors in the US but by holding companies controlled by GM in Spain. For the German government to un-bundle this conglomerate will be very hard to do.

That's why Peter Bofinger, one of the *"Fünf Weisen"* (five wise) economic advisors as the leading economists in Germany advising the chancellor are referred to suggested not to guarantee for Opel but rather to nationalise the company and get it out of the claws of the collapsing mother company, GM.

The US government which now holds a majority stake in GM could have cut a deal with Magna which the German government had favored. It came at the end of a state dinner upon Chancellor Merkel's visit on 3rd November 2008 that an advisor told her that the CEO of GM had rung to tell that the Magna deal was called off. Quite embarrassing for both, Mr. Obama as well as Mrs. Merkel. It has transpired that these car manufacturers only have gotten into trouble because its management had gambled in the casinos of the financial markets and lost a billion Dollars per month each. In case of Opel it is even more severe: most of the technological development of GM is done in Rüsselsheim near Frankfurt am Main. Those jobs are at stake once GM closes down.

The effects are already felt elsewhere: BASF, Germany's major chemical company sends 5,000 workers home – into early Christmas holidays. The declining demand by car makers resulted in a slowdown in chemical products such as paint.

Many other companies, SMEs especially, are affected by the economic decline of the German car industry.

Fear goes around that the collapse of the American economy will bring down Germany as well. To propose at this time that Germany prove its European commitment by putting up money for the EU Commission's support-package is somewhat ludicrous. Germany, no matter how much its leadership have in good times advocated European integration is not standing by its foes in bad times, it seems.

All the EU leaders are now able to agree on is that everyone looks after himself.

AN APOLOGY

I apologise and correct myself. Having written about food inflation and bio fuel as well recently I have to correct some of the allegations I held against the ethanol industry. In a full page advert in the Financial Times a world leading ethanol company goes into the offensive.

It is not nice to be blamed for all the evil in the world and especially not so if one might subjectively feel wrongly accused.

Those who should rather be blamed are our democratically elected political leaders allowing these corporations to engage in what they are doing.

In its advertisement *Abengoa Bionenergy* cites that "EU food price inflation increased 4.7% year-on-year in October 2008 while corn and wheat prices dropped more than 50% from a year ago" quoting Eurostat's EU Food Price Index (HICP).

Part of the previous hike has been due to financial speculation and the bio-ethanol producers are not to be made responsible for that. As the financial bubbles were seeking another playground after the sub-prime mortgage market collapsed these vagabonding 4,500 billion dollars briefly went into the food commodity market, and created an energy- and alternative energy bubble.

As a consequence prices for food were soaring. But, as food is a commodity which can not be kept on stock for an indefinite or even long period like precious metals or some fossil fuel products the speculators went elsewhere. Logically, food prices dropped again.

With the final crash coming closer every day now there are less and less playgrounds for the virtual reality - wealth.

INADVERTENTLY THE AD PROVES THAT OIL AND FOOD PRICES ARE LINKED

The argument that "cereal prices decreased 50% in the past 12 month while EU ethanol production doubled over the same period" as the advert claims does not make the case for bio-fuel but is rather evidence that oil and food prices are tied.

If oil prices fall, bio-fuel production declines. On the contrary, if oil prices soar, more ethanol is produced and food scarcity rises. It is funny that the statistics quoted in the advert inadvertently proves exactly that.

Oil and bio-fuel prices are linked. Oil prices went down because of the financial crisis and so did food prices. Oil prices will go up again, soon because demand steadily increases while production becomes more expensive as peak oil point has been reached this year.

But, this means that hunger is subject to speculation. When oil prices go up, ethanol prices go up, too. Logically, food prices soar as well. Thus the hungry in the world are played against the interests of the ethanol industry.

The facts show that the ethanol industry's argument is rather cynical as although bio-fuel may not be directly made responsible for food inflation it nevertheless takes away food from the hungry.

This being said one should not forget that also energy corporations like the car industry heavily participated in the crazy financial speculation that brought industries down and led to speculation in all kinds of commodities.

It is a fact that two tank fillings of a medium sized car with bio-fuel require the amount of corn equal to what a child could live on for one year. Could, yes, but if said child lives in poverty it cannot create a sufficient market demand, or better: the demand would be there but the purchasing power may be absent.

That's why it is correct to say that bio-fuel is not responsible for food inflation although price developments can be linked to it as even the advert tells us.

6 OF THE WORLD'S 10 MAJOR CORPORATIONS ARE ENERGY CONGLOMERATES

Nevertheless, we could do something more sensible than fuelling our cars: feed a human being. Food scarcity is not a result from economic givens only but also a result from a lack of democracy.

As long as multinational corporations (6 of the world's major 10 are energy conglomerates) can dictate their conditions and prices, there is no room for democracy. These multinational energy conglomerates don't care about by what they make their profit, be it fossil fuel or ethanol.

For as long as their shareholder's value imposes a brutal profit maximisation, food will go into the tanks of our cars and no democratically elected representative will be able to stop this craziness as it is built into our present economic system like the financial market - casinos had been into it until recently, too.

If only one had stopped the free-market apologists in time, one could have averted the present crisis. But, to demand that was not feasible as politicians who tried it were isolated, ridiculed and even punished while journalists who covered such attempts all of a sudden were not printed or put on air anymore.

The energy industry did better to change course, abandon bio-fuel and save their money for these expensive ads as democracy will teach them that an image campaign won't do. Eastern European socialists had to learn it the hard way, too. "Those who come too late are punished by life", former Soviet President Mikhail S. Gorbachev had told us in 1989 and couldn't escape the same fate himself.

LET'S TALK ABOUT HUNGER AND DEMOCRACY

A sustainable economic model would not allow livestock be fed from cropland that could grow edible food forcing hundreds of millions of human beings to go hungry since half of the world's grain is fed nowadays to livestock.

What if the other half is soon to be used to fuel our cars?

The same applies to the world's fish supply. By feeding fish to fish, the potential supply is shrinking. Corn and grain become filet mignon, sardines become salmon. The reason for this is that people in poor countries are not seen as a market creating a sufficient demand for the fruits of the earth or the fish in our seas. That's why only the rich countries can afford it, the poor starve.

Every ten seconds a child dies of hunger.

To say that bio-fuel is not the *direct* reason for food inflation is right. But to conclude from that that there wasn't sufficient demand for food is missing the point and is simply cynical.

Democracy is at stake if we let shareholder value continue to rule over us.

EU Commission and European Parliament could have decided democratically to force these companies to abstain from exploiting the talk about climate change for their goals.

But maybe lobbying has been too overwhelming for our democratically elected leaders in order to come to a wise conclusion. What happens when things get out of hand when political leaders govern against the majority of people had been observed in Greece at the end of 2008 when student protests illuminated Athens for several days. So far it is not the hungry of this world that come to riot in Brussels or other European and American headquarters yet.

Good for the Financial Times to have the advertisement income from these industries. One can only hope that the colleague's editorial position won't suffer from that.

VI.

THE GREAT DEPRESSION –
THIS TIME IN
TECHNICOLOR

European industries across the board are in a sharp decline. The worldwide economic crisis once more took it's beginning in the US. But, why are German, British, South Korean and Japanese carmakers and other manufacturers so terribly hit? And, is it really as bad as 80 years ago? The most significant difference may be that in 1929, the US had been the largest creditor, today it is the largest debtor; however, the outcome may be the same due to structural flaws of the economic system. Americans and Europeans are sitting in the same boat, not the same life-raft, though. And, the disaster is a result from mismanagement by those who think that when being bailed out by governments that it only requires a bit of fine-tuning in order to bring things back on track and keep on trucking. This, basically, is the approach EU Commission and EU Council are taking.

History doesn't repeat itself, but there are always periods which show similarities, some of these frightening, some encouraging ones. The explosive mixture of the crisis of 1929 which resulted in the Great Depression bringing bitter poverty and hunger back into industrialised nations which led to World War II consisted of 5 major components which may ring a bell for us, too:

In the pretext of 1929 there has been a huge imbalance of income distribution. The concentration of income at the top of society crippled domestic demand.

This re-distribution of wealth from bottom to top of society resulted from the gains of an increased productivity. US productivity per employee rose by 43% between 1919 and 1929 but it had only been transferred to the profit share while wages stagnated.

Secondly, this effect got enhanced by generous tax breaks by which the US government, like in recent years, had pampered the upper class. Domestic demand foremost increased by the consumption of luxury goods while GDP growth solely consisted of investment in the investment goods industry which in the 20ies still grew annually by some 6.5%.

The investment in the capital goods sector had been much less significant which led to a shrinking consumption share. When in 1929 investment into capital goods due to overcapacities lost its dynamism the crash that followed *stante pede* spoilt the party for the upper class.

The third reason for the Great Depression to spread ever faster in the 1930ies was the swindles and bluffs by holding companies and investment trusts which orchestrated a firework of mergers and takeovers. Although superfluous capital got absorbed and by this increased the return on investment, mega corporations - being producing- and financial conglomerates under the same roof counting endless layers - dominated the markets.

These monsters naturally had no interest in innovation and development as speculation promised a higher return. On top of that, the impenetrable structure of such 'Russian puppet'- corporations made manipulations of the balance sheets, by which profits could fictionally be pushed upwards, extremely easy.

Much more severe in fact was that the Enron's, WorldCom's, Lehman Brothers, Merrill Lynch's and Goldman Sachs' of that period created financial pyramids which because they included the producing industry in their structures took these with them into the grave when collapsing.

Investment-Trusts back then, like Hedge Funds today, posed as the fourth evil requiring high returns from the companies they owned in order to finance the interest payments for the credits they took for their speculation. But, ever higher returns are only achievable by one-time – effects such as cutting down on wages, social expenditure as well as investments, the latter which once more strangles the economic dynamism.

Lastly, the fifth major reason for the collapse of the economic system of that time is to be seen in the fact that after WWI the US had posed as the largest creditor on the world's financial markets. Today it is the largest debtor. Other than nowadays, in the 1920ies the US exported much more than it imported. The surpluses were financed by an influx of gold and silver. In addition, German bonds were greatly appreciated by the American upper class to have otherwise superfluous liquidity being absorbed.

With a bit of sarcasm one can say that these American bonds served to a large degree the reparations payment of the German government. The money Americans invested in German bonds only virtually travelled to Germany. De facto – as WWI reparation payment

– it ended up in Uncle Sam's deep pockets. The US government badly needed those funds for paying interests for its own bonds, which, and this is quite amusing, benefited exactly those people who had signed for German government bonds as well.

One may not find it tragic that the American upper class by this absurd cycle paid itself interest but the problem was that this huge imbalance of vagabonding funds seeking investment opportunities on the one hand and the enormous debt on the other became a self enhancing mechanism.

Like in any other chain-letter or Ponzi-financing scheme it has been clear that the debt will never be paid back. We are today in a similar situation, although diametrically reversed as this time it is the US which is the debtor, but the huge imbalances are of same magnitude and the crashes inevitable no matter how much bailout-packages are put on the table.

It is not a specifically American problem. The fatal consequences of an economic system which' manufacturing industries are dying a silent death while weapons and derivatives have become the main export goods are not a mere coincidence. They are the result of the wrong path of development also we in Europe are marching down since the late 1990ies.

We are not better than the Americans, we only started later and for that reason our economies haven't degenerated as much, yet. The advantage we Europeans could benefit from is that we still have the chance to reverse history's course.

EU IN RECESSION: LIVING FROM HAND TO MOUTH

Transatlantic quarrels over how to solve the crisis are to continue. While German car makers are worst hit by the American decline all other export leaning industries in Europe suffer tremendously from the economic downturn. EU leaders try to impose their way, but US aren't ready for real change. President Nicolas Sarkozy seems to engage in right-wing Socialism he may wish to win the US administration for.

No matter how much the world celebrated the election of Barack Obama there should be no misunderstanding about whose president the charismatic leader will be. President Obama serves the American people and uses his charm to push through the interest of whatever is deemed to be in the interest of the United States of America and rightly so.

We Europeans shouldn't be naïve: a regulated financial market IMF president Dominique Strauss-Kahn and French President Nicolas Sarkozy envision is not in the interest of the US or those who stand behind Wall Street. The Obama-administration won't give up the American economic model that easily.

A closer scrutiny of the development of global financial wealth reveals that in the past 25 years the volume of financial wealth has grown much faster than nominal GDP. Between 1980 and 2005 the investment in any kind of financial instruments, be it Commercial Debt Obligations (CDOs) or bonds of privately owned companies has multiplied by the factor 20.

This newly accumulated wealth has been used to finance the purchase of ever more obligations and stocks.

Largest beneficiary of this development have been owners and shareholders of US companies. But, also public debt has, after a longer period of stagnation in the 1990ies, exploded.

The US' financial markets created a constant influx of foreign capital. This off-set their massive imports. The trade deficit is enormous. Main US exports in the past three decades have been dubious financial instruments and treasury bonds by which domestic consumption and standard of living were financed.

Even if President Barack Obama wanted to depart from this sick economic model, the question would remain how would he maintain the standard of living for the great majority of American households? He should re-industrialise the US, but that will take time. Other than debts there is not much left over from the dotcom hype of the Clinton-Gore years.

When speaking of a financial bubble one should not only mention the stock markets, financial markets and hedge funds which got into trouble but also the excessive public and private indebtedness. The latter has grown in the past 25 years many times bigger than the real economy's growth.

The debt-bubble which started to build up during the 80ies and 90ies had reached an unimaginable volume. It has been the direct consequence of an ever increased profit maximisation and capital amortisation.

This is especially so because the neo-liberal agenda of wage-dumping, cracking down on social standards and granting tax relief to ultra rich and major corporations only reduces the costs of production but can hardly solve the problem of creating profitable demand since the declining purchasing power makes any self-sustaining investment dynamism impossible.

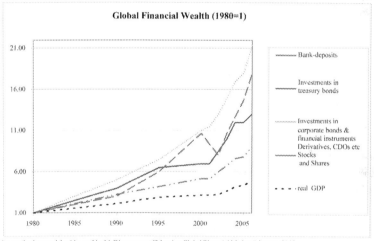

Source for data used for this graphic: McKinsey report "Mapping Global Financial Markets" January 2008

Any economic policy which seriously is inclined to increase the return on investment and capital amortisation needs to provide the frame for an ever-lasting growth of demand from either one of the four potential wells: upper-class consumption, credit financed state expenditure, consumer indebtedness or export.

Different countries were granting different priority status to these four components but whatever has been the highest priority all of the aforementioned forms to increase demand produced and always will produce this financial foam that surmounts the real (producing) economy.

It is because every credit issued to state or consumers inadvertently leads to a pyramid of debts on the one side and a bubble of financial wealth - even if it is only on paper or stored electronically - on the other side. This follows the same logic like lasting export surpluses of one state require to have deficits by other countries on the opposite side.

Also, the subsidizing of luxury consumption in the US has been based primarily on speculative capital gains which the companies had financed by an ever increasing indebtedness.

The US had lived quite well by that scheme. It allowed the US to pay for their imports by worthless paper. Once this system is led ad absurdum supply won't match demand in any way anymore. US citizens will have to tighten their belts.

Logic, that the owners of Wall Street who had to a large degree supported Mr. Obama's campaign won't agree with him changing the rules of the game completely by letting international institutions regulate and control what used to work so damned well for so long.

The infamous term "credit crunch" takes a different meaning as it is not only the financial crisis which is responsible for the breaking down of the inter-bank lending market. The problem is much deeper rooted. It is the constant struggle of finding a balance between supply and demand, credit and debts, import and export, haves and have-not's. The French right-wing Socialistic approach will only be populism as the real issues aren't dealt with.

THE ,S'- CURVE

That our present system is as rotten as the past socialism becomes obvious when one scrutinises the supply – demand relation. Never before did industries produce such an incredible amount of low quality goods, useless or superfluous products and trash.

It has become obvious in the 1930ies that the mixture of free markets and unlimited capital accumulation had been explosive. Its apologists for the next 40 years had a hard stance. Keynesianism has been the logic conclusion drawn from WWII.

It suggested that the state created a regulatory framework and if necessary also the necessary domestic demand. This seemed to work quite well in the 50ies and 60ies of last century. But, it has been the capitalistic investment dynamic that enhanced the post-war prosperity, driven by the need of reconstruction, distribution of new mass-manufactured goods as well as a general consumption desire.

Continuous wage increases, a pre-requirement for rising consumption shares, under the above conditions had been no threat to increasing profit rates because the rapid rise of productivity due to automated production lines gave room for a generous distribution of wealth.

In economic theory the development of the demand curve is often referred to as the 'S' curve. At the beginning only a few people bought washing machines and refrigerators but as soon as wages increased more and more households could afford the new luxury. The curve steeply leads upwards. Finally, washing machines and refrigerators are part of a general standard.

Now, mostly young people or people whose fridge got broken buy one. The demand curve is almost flat. Then, with new variations and improved versions of already successfully introduced products such as washing machines with 10 instead of 5 programs and centrifuges or mobile phones with internet connectivity the curve lets the curve go up again.

The 'S' curve is *the* dominant analogy of demand driven economies. The rapid growth of demand along the steeper parts of the curve stimulates above average investments in order to create the required capacities. Because one concludes from the present demand what the future holds in store it is quite common that an investment – overkill creates overcapacities.

A market cleansing due to overcapacities kicks those who came too late out of business.

During the post WWII era an extraordinary amount of products all of a sudden became mass-manufactured goods which required huge investments for creating the necessary production capacities. A company which intends to double its car manufactory's output requires to have considerable more investment goods than a company which wants to supply the double amount of mobile phones.

The expansion of capacities of European companies in the post war era by this had also been an important stimulant for the US as the American companies at the beginning had been the only ones who could provide investment goods. However, in the due course, the European companies seeking investment goods inadvertently became rivals of the American corporations supplying same kind of goods.

Simultaneously, the upper end of the 'S' curve of standard goods of the industrialised societies had been reached in the late sixties. The worldwide created capacities under profit share and return-on-investment aspects had been much too big. The competition on the world market sharpened up and profit rates declined.

Much too much capital had been invested in creating these capacities which yet had to amortise before the corporations could change the field of business. The investments declined sharply and for a while could no longer pose as a well for profitable demand.

This constellation, and not currency turbulences and the oil price shock, had been the deeper rooted reason for the first worldwide economic crisis after WWII.

In the western free world this challenge was met by a dreadful financial deregulation binding capital in useless speculations along with mass production of junk products and trash. In the Socialistic east the attempt to keep pace with capitalistic production output choked the command economy.

Whereas Socialism promised that one will get all one needed Capitalism until today seems to promise that we will need all we are getting.

VII.

WARSHIPPING THE SCAPEGOAT

A NEW CHAPTER IN *THE GREAT GAME*

It was on the last day of February of 2008 that the International Energy Agency (IEA) in Paris had warned of an unprecedented energy crisis that will hit the global economy in the next four years and which is believed to carry worse effects than the present economic crisis.

Ironically, one reason for the upcoming energy shortage is the currently extreme low oil price that discourages major energy conglomerates from investing into exploration of new fields.

It could become a tragic moment to see the world economy struggle to get out of crisis and be let's ay half way out of it just to be then hit by hyper inflation in the oil market because of shortages.

That's why the IEA demands that the major corporations (6 of the world top 10 are energy corporations) to invest otherwise a price of 200 Dollars per barrel (it was 140 Dollars in the last summer and now tumbles around 40 Dollars) could cripple a slowly recovering economy in 2013 as IEA Director Nobuo Tanaka warned.

This of course is not much more than breathing down the neck of these energy conglomerates. The present crisis has proven that privately owned companies only invest when an immediate profit can be achieved.

Ralph T. Niemeyer

FINAL FIGHT OVER RESOURCES

Long-term perspectives are only playing a role if substantial returns can be expected which in regards to oil are unlikely as Climate Change defined goals of reducing emissions force the industry to rather invest into alternative energy which due to economic crisis and a pathologic focussing on the revival of nuclear energy is also neglected.

At the same time the fight over already explored oil and gas fields intensifies. Whereas Russia sees its hegemony been put into jeopardy by NATO expansion to Georgia and Central Asia as well as Ukraine, the EU Commission entered the pipeline-poker on 27th January 2009 in Budapest.

The consortia for the long-planned Nabucco pipeline consisting of Austrian OMV, German RWE, Hungarian MOL, Rumanian Transgaz, Turkish Botas and Bulgarian Bulgargaz jumpstarted the project by the European Investment Bank (EIB) to guarantee to fund a quarter of the construction costs with Commission President José Manuel Barroso pledging 250 million Euros.

Nabucco will shun Russia in channelling gas and oil from the Caspian Sea region to the West. A third of the world's natural gas reserves are located in the Caspian Sea. On Russian territory a constant decline is noted. At present, the EU imports 60% of its annual energy consumption of which 40% come from Russia.

It is estimated that in the next two decades EU consumption will increase to 80% of the consumed natural gas. In 2020 some 509 billion cubic metres of gas will have to be imported into the EU.

Countries such as Iran, Azerbaijan, Turkmenistan as direct neighbours to the Caspian Sea but also Georgia, the US and Russia are the main rivals in the poker over the hegemony in the region.

Germany as a close ally and friend of Russia plays a special role in so far as the planned North-Stream pipeline from Russia to Germany through the Baltic Sea shunning Poland, ex Soviet Baltic republics and Sweden shows the intensity of the Russian – German cooperation.

The Polish government is said to be quite upset about Berlin actively hindering EU co-financing of Polish energy projects in order to break the resistance of Warsaw against the North-Stream pipeline. The German energy providers E.on and BASF were awarded participation agreements in Russian gas exploration while in exchange Gazprom bought itself into the German gas infrastructure.

Siemens AG just recently formed an alliance with the Russian nuclear energy consortium Rosatom in order to play a more dominant international role.

Above facts can be seen as a contradiction to other German interests in the Central Asian region. RWE chairman Jürgen Großmann visited the Despot Gurbanguly Berdymuchammedov in Turkmenistan to sign long-term supply contracts. Little later, at that time EU Council President, the Czech Minister-president Mirek Topolanek visited in Ashgabat the autocratic Berdymuchammedov who suddenly advanced in Western media to "President Berdymuchammedov" although he was so far always portrayed as a dictator.

Russia's answer to the EU's 'confrontational cooperation' is another pipeline: the so called South-Stream project which is a clear alternative to the Nabucco pipeline as it shall be laid on the ground of the Black Sea from Russia to Bulgaria and supply South Eastern and Central Europe by shunning Ukraine.

Last August's war between Georgia and Russia can be seen in the light of a growing nervousness in the region as the cards are dealt anew.

ANOTHER PROXY WAR

The EU is split over the Gaza conflict. The Czech EU Presidency was outmanoeuvred by French President Nicolas Sarkozy who unlike his counterpart in Prague, Vaclav Klaus, pursues a moderate policy in the conflict.

The World seems to be taken by surprise by the Christmas Day - insurgence of Israel in Gaza but Russian security advisors have warned about it for quite some time. I had learnt from an advisor to Russian President Vladimir Medvedev speaking on condition of anonymity in July 2008 about a strategy allegedly orchestrated by the US and Israel targeting Iran.

Would an US-Israeli trained army in Georgia launch an attack against South Ossetia in order to provoke an over-reaction by Russia?

Would the international outcry allow for the US to strengthen its presence in Georgia and use its territory as a major base for a potential war against Iran in case Israel feels threatened by the Mullah regime? Before 7th August 2008 such scenario was put down to conspiracy theories.

All bullocks? Said high ranking Russian security advisor had warned more than half a year ago that the Bush-White House and oil giants would try to fix things before Barack Obama would be inaugurated. Today we know that Israel had planned the ground offensive in Gaza for some 18 months.

Hamas, although democratically legitimated, has throughout its existence been supported and financed by Iran. British Channel Four had invited Iranian President Ahmadi-Nedjad to deliver an address which outraged the public although he fell short of launching any verbal attacks against Israel.

It may only be a matter of days or weeks until Iran becomes directly involved, one can fear.

Besides the ongoing conflict which has its roots in 3000 years of history there are other, important geo-strategic components, to be reported:

According to said Russian security advisor the Baku-Tbilissi-Ceyhan oil pipeline and the Nabucco - gas-pipeline from the Caspian Sea to Vienna leading through Georgia by this form an integral part of the US dominated energy corridor, sidelining Russia but also shunning Iran. It speaks for itself but not for him that former German Foreign Minister Joseph ("Joschka") Fischer, a *Green-Pacifist*, who advocated the Kosovo and Afghanistan wars as well as a German engagement in the Iraq war, is nowadays working for the Nabucco consortium. It all makes sense now that this man ordered to bomb Serbia as President Milosevic had resisted the attempts by the West to lay a pipeline across Yugoslavian territory sidelining Russia.

A look on the global geo-strategic network the United States have spun around Russia and Central Asia makes it clear why Georgia is of such vital importance to the West:

From Barents Sea in the North of Norway to Kotzebue at the Bering's Strait in Northwest Alaska the ring of the US – Western circle reaches around Russia via Finland to the Baltic Republics, Poland, Ukraine, Turkey, Iraq, Afghanistan and Japan.

The big gap in this global hegemony, China, is also surrounded even though it is neither complete nor stable enough to ensure sustainability. The militarization of the trade routes justified by the "fight against pirates" as well as the collapse of Pakistan after the Mumbai-attacks provides for the perfect excuse for new troop deployments in those regions.

The massive US investment over almost 2 decades into building up this hegemony will guarantee a good return, President Medvedev's advisor told me.

There is still a huge gap at the South – Western flank of Russia Washington is said to be eager to close between Caucasus and Caspian Sea which is rich in resources. Georgia's war over South-Ossetia is seen by Russia as the United States' attempt to close this gap.

Likewise, the Russian government interprets the US-Israeli investment into infrastructure in the transport corridor that stretches from Baku in Azerbaijan via Georgia to the Kurdish-Turkish port of Ceyhan at the Mediterranean Sea as preparations for an upcoming war against Iran.

The 5,000 metres high Caucasus is strategically important for Russia as well as any other power that wishes to control the region, I was told.

When at the end of last century the Russian Republic of Chechnya - with the help from the West and Saudi Arabia conquered the neighbouring Republic of Dagestan a major war has been imminent but averted because Russia was lulled-in by Pro-Western bankers and government officials under President Yeltsin.

And, when Georgian soldiers, trained by US- and Israeli specialists, had invaded the Russian domain of Southern Ossetia in August 2008, Abkhazian troops made use of the opportunity of the moment by re-conquering the upper Kodori valley with its pass over the Tchalta mountains to Karatchajevo-Tcherkessia which all along has been Russian territory.

Much more southern of the Caucasian mountains, Russia has ever since good supporters in the Armenians who had prevailed in the wars at the end of the Soviet Union over Nagorny Karabach.

The shortest land connection to South Asia would be through Iran whose major gas reserves are more or less untouched. But, as long as the US haven't sorted out the Iran issue in their favour, all transport corridors either lead through Russia which doesn't suit US interests or across the Caucasus.

There is already a pipeline from Baku through Chechnya to the Russian Novorossik at the Black Sea, but since rebels had interrupted such, the Russian were forced to lay a bypass through Dagestan.

An Israeli news service, DEBKAfile, had reported that Israeli capital as well as the government is interested in the oil and gas pipelines through Georgia.

According to this information, Israel had proposed Turkey to extend the Tbilisi-Ceyhan pipeline through the Mediterranean to Ashkelon in Israel. Through this trans-Israel pipeline oil and gas could be transported to Eilat at the Red Sea and from there to South Asia while the Iranian reserves (once Iran is "freed") could be tapped from there.

Initially, Israel had hoped to win the Russians as investors as well as suppliers but Vladimir Putin showed a cold shoulder to the Israelis and shook hands with Iran's President Mahmoud Ahmadinejad, a man who rules by means of the death penalty against leftists, instead. And, President Medvedev reaffirmed Russian – Indian ties only days after the Mumbai attacks leasing nuclear submarines to India.

The Israel-US-friendly government in Georgia seems to be the last stakeholder in the region for those two nations. The anger over the rockets fired from Hamas can rather be seen as a welcome excuse to draw Iran ever deeper into the conflict than a real threat to Israel's existence. At least that's the point of view of the Russian government.

SHOWDOWN AT THE HORN OF AFRICA

The militarization of yet another trade route adds to the new East-West confrontation as does the UN war crimes tribunal to a growing

North – South conflict. Meanwhile Moscow and Beijing shore up their cooperation on a 25 billion Dollars pipeline project. And, in last December India and Russia vowed to cooperate on security issues with Russia 'leasing out' 8 nuclear submarines to India while the Western Alliance, NATO, concluded on March 5 that it's troops will be deployed also in Pakistan as Secretary of State Rodham Clinton pointed out.[30]

Although German foreign Minister Frank Walter Steinmeier told me that NATO involvement in Sudan "was not an issue", (see video link) the hunt for pirates suggests something rather different.

The waters around Somalia have seen the biggest gathering of international marine vessels in history. Besides war ships from US and Europe, also Russia, India and foremost China are represented. In total more than 20 countries are claiming their stakes. A different kind of G20 gathering one could say.

Officially, this is for the sake of civil maritime business and its protection against pirates and/or terrorists who are said to have their bases along the 3,300 kilometres long coast.

One may wonder, though, what the enormous costs of the military protection of the Gulf of Aden (so far more than 500 million Euros have been spent) are justified with. The total of all ransom being paid had been far less than 100 million Dollars. The German foreign aid to the starving population of Somalia in 2007 was less than 10 million Euros, but the military budget of Germany reserved 43.1 million Euros for EU lead *Operation Atalanta* fighting against piracy during this year.

One reason for the increase of piracy in the region is to be seen in the industrialised over-fishing in the gulf that ruined the Somali fishers and hardly left them with any choice but to make a living from criminal activity. Another reason is, of course, the fact that for the past 15 years there is no real functioning government in Somalia. A mafia-like organised international scene of dumpers of contaminated waste also make use of the deep sea at the Horn of Africa.

A World Bank program to help Somali fishers was revoked after the IMF abandoned all efforts to help Somalia rebuild it's statehood after a devastating civil war. Some 400 Soldiers who had not been paid by their government anymore also joined the pirates. Under these

---

30 http://www.facebook.com/home.php?#/video/video.
php?v=69272238581&ref=nf

conditions, it is ludicrous for the Western Alliance to demand from Somalia to police the trade route.

But the massive presence of navies from around the globe can hardly be explained by some unemployed and frustrated fisherman capering oil tankers. It rather seems to have to do with another area of mutual interest of the G20: the oil of neighbouring Sudan.

It has become evident that China was secretly financing some of the Islamic rebel groups which are aligned with the Sudanese government.

The Chinese magazine "China business" in it's May 2007 edition clearly pointed out what in reality the issue was about: "Darfur: forget about the killings, there is oil." According to this article there was (since the Iraq invasion) a new cold war between China and the US over the control of the oil resources.

According to this article also in Chad and Sudan the two countries are rivals.

Since 2006 Sudan is the fourth largest oil supplier for China which buys 80% of the oil produced in Southern Sudan. China's oil concession in South Sudan concerns block 6 which directly borders with Darfur.

After the Sudanese government had announced in 2005 that there was also oil found in South Darfur, all of a sudden rebel groups financed from abroad popped up and stirred the conflict.

Forces from neighbouring Ethiopia invaded the country which since more than 15 years had not had a normal statehood. The so called *Islamic Courts,* sponsored by China, were seen by the majority of the population as a stabilising factor and not as *Jihadists* harbouring al Qaeda terrorists, but as those bringing the ordeal of the previous 15 years of fighting between warlords and clans to an end by defeating them within 6 months.

UN Resolution 1725 instigated by the US who rallied for weeks as usual citing al - Qaeda connections thus justifying military intervention opened the door for Ethiopian troops in December 2006. In mid January of 2007 the US bombed Southern Somali "terrorist targets". There was no evidence that among the 50 civilian casualties there has been any al Qaeda terrorist.

"China Business" accuses the US to prepare an intervention by NATO after a failed mission by the Organisation of African Union (OAU) that seems to deliberately be given a weak mandate.

The delay of the UN hybrid forces along with disappearing EU funds which did not reach the OAU troops and by this further undermined their commitment can be seen as creating a justification for a more robust intervention by NATO – all in the good and honourable aim to rescue innocent lives.

The International War Crimes Tribunal in The Hague that issued an international arrest warrant against Sudan's authoritarian leader Omar Hassan al Baschir which is widely ignored by the African nations but also by Russia and China is facing a debacle when veto powers question the legitimacy of the UN court.

This may happen, soon as EUreporter was told in Moscow by a high government official who spoke on condition of anonymity. The War Crimes Tribunal is seen as serving interests of the West the source told EUreporter referring to the US' special role in having championed the court while declining to grant it any power when it comes to US suspects. "The court has been remarkably silent when it came to US rendition flights and torture camps in Poland, Romania, Iraq and Afghanistan of which some still exist" the source told EUreporter "so why should Africa recognise it?".

It becomes clearer every day that the ongoing slaughtering of civilians in Sudan as well as the fight against pirates will only serve as an excuse for military interventions in the region.

European corporations are already sitting on the sidelines once the secession of Sudan has been manifested: The German Thyssen-Krupp along with other major European industries who through the European Roundtable of Industrialists (ERT) for quite some time lobbied the EU Commission to secure their bid on the Darfur region expects some 8 billion Euros in revenues from investments into the region according to the German financial daily *Handelsblatt* commenting on the German Bundeswehr's new *Weissbuch* in which the new "international character of the German forces' task" is laid out.

One of the goals openly mentioned in the *Weissbuch* shall be to secure the "free and unhindered world trade, securing of the transport corridors as well as a stabile energy subsistence".

BLACK GOLD TO BE TREASURED

Reporting from Moscow

The prophesy has been out there for quite some time, but it never seemed to happen: Oil exploration has peaked this month as for the first time since 2003 oil production has not increased. At the same time oil prices fell to little more than 40 Dollars per barrel which is largely owed to the global economic downturn.

But, oil prices are likely to soar in the near future again despite a decreasing demand. Not a contradiction if one reads a study of the German geological institute *Bundesanstalt für Geowissenschaften und Rohstoffe* a government body which comes to the conclusion that within the next 12 years half of the world's economically exploitable oil reserves will be used up.

This analysis is shared by Pat Howell, the drilling supervisor of LUKoil, the Russian major oil producing company. Mr. Howell, an American engineer working on Siberian sites some 230 days a year for the past 10 years says that not only had it been predictable to anyone in the business but also widely expected.

Exploration becomes ever more expensive Mr. Howell explains because one has to drill ever deeper. On the other hand, demand is only slowing down but not really retracting as East Asian emerging economies will make good for the decline put down to the recession in industrialised countries hit by the financial crisis.

That's why for the years to come LUKoil will still explore new oil fields even in adverse weather conditions in Siberia but it's commitment got a time-expiration on it. For the time being all will be fine.

Thereafter it will become increasingly difficult and expensive to explore new wells. Production will decline significantly, the study says. Peak-Oil-Point has been reached.

At the end of 2006 a total of 163.7 billion barrels of worldwide economically exploitable oil resources had been recorded, followed by 163.5 billion barrels in 2007. In the past the annual study of the institute has always predicted an increase in oil production so in this sense the present study is unprecedented in saying that there will be less output.

And, it is true: last year the world's oil production fell from 3.92 billion barrel in 2006 to 3.88 billion barrel in 2007. The fact that this number has not dropped more significantly yet is due to much more advanced technology otherwise the figures would point downwards.

Although the economic crisis is slowing down industrial production worldwide the introduction of western lifestyle in Asian emerging markets will always create sufficient demand even if the Chinese economy is slowing down, too.

Double digit growth rates won't be seen for the years to come but still there will be growth in India and China which will probably make up for the decreasing demand from Western industrialised nations.

Ironically, one could say that the Chinese and Indian populations are increasingly driving cars while our recession in this market will rather suggest that we will ride bicycles.

THE ACTUAL TOLL OF THE MUMBAI-ATTACKS

Reporting from Moscow.

President Medvedev had visited India just days after the Mumbai attacks. He had met with President Singh in order to enhance the relationship.

As trade between the two nations is expected to have risen by 2 billion in 2008 to 7 billion Dollars there is also an intensified military cooperation to be noticed.

Although India was a bit disappointed by the delay of the delivery of a new aircraft carrier which Moscow has postponed until 2012 cooperation in other fields gains ground.

Russia is assisting India in building 4 nuclear power stations.

It also comes as no surprise that Russia reassures India of its commitment to fight terrorism. In the aftermath of the Mumbai attacks the Indian government has been, behind closed doors, been told by the US government that they wished to see a solution be agreed on within 48 hours, I learnt from a source close to President Medvedev.

Besides the human toll, the terrorists are also responsible for attacking the economy of a country which was still growing while others are nearing depression.

RUSSIA WORRIED ABOUT TROUBLES AT NEW "US'S BORDER WITH INDIA"

What sounds as if the US were coming out in support of India in fact is interpreted differently in Delhi as a senior Russian official told EUreporter. "It was seen as an ultimatum. If India was not willing to cooperate with the US in shutting down terror camps in neighbouring Pakistan and also solve the Kashmir conflict, the US would do so by themselves" the source told EUreporter.

This would mean that US would withdraw more troops from Afghanistan were the incoming Obama administration is insisting on an increased European engagement and shift those to the Pakistani-Indian border.

Russia expressing suspicion on the merits of US presence in Georgia is eager to stake its claim, too as the entire region could be destabilized with the two major energy corridors being affected, too.

President Medvedev made clear that the focus of his visit was on defence-ties: "We are also talking about cooperation in the sphere of leasing atomic submarines" the Russian president said.

It has become clear that after the Mumbai – 9/11 which took a human toll of 171 India is trying hard to keep the economic toll of the still growing market to a minimum while keeping the Americans at bay.

They could become neighbours if one is considering Pakistan a 'failed state'. The cards of the strategic energy poker game have just been dealt anew.

UKRAINE SPLIT-UP NEAR?

Ukrainian Prime Minister Julya Tymochenko and EU Commission president José Manuel Barroso agreed in March 2009 that the door for Ukrainian EU membership shall remain open amid some difficulties between pro Russian and pro Western groups in Ukraine.

Also, IMF, World Bank and European Investment Bank (EIB) shall help the country.

That would sound nice if there wasn't a catch. After the repeated conflicts over the gas supply from Russia any such multilateral talks are designed to further stir the conflict rather than putting it to rest if Russia is excluded from these consultations.

EU Commission President José Manuel Barroso made it clear what the Conference on Modernisation of Ukraine's Gas Transit was about:

"I am very glad to say that the Commission, the Government of Ukraine and representatives of three international financial institutions, the EIB, EBRD and the World Bank will shortly sign a joint declaration to move forward together on the key tasks of reforming the Ukraine gas sector to bring it into the EU's internal energy market and for modernising the Ukraine gas transit network."

ENERGY CONFERENCE IN BRUSSELS HELD WITHOUT RUSSIA

The latter is certainly necessary especially since Russia is said to be reluctant to invest into the Ukrainian network after the conflict in which both sides accused each other by not adhering to the contracts. Understandable, but the conference had been agreed to well before the latest dispute between Russia and Ukraine.

EU Commission President Barroso told me that "this conference has been planned more than 10 months ago" and was in no way directed against Russia.

But, Russian Prime Minister Vladimir Putin immediately reacted mocking the EU-Ukrainian "gas summit" calling it ludicrous to sign agreements over modernising pipelines without the actual supplier. "What are these pipelines worth without our gas?" he asked.

Russia's two pipeline projects Northstream leading through the Baltic Sea bypassing all Ex- Soviet Republics and Poland, and Southsteam on the bed of the Black Sea shunning Bulgaria and Romania can be seen as an attempt to cut-out middlemen.

Despite the gas dispute there is another, more internal rather than international conflict between Russia and Ukraine arising, that about who will control the Ukrainian steel industry in the future.

Like other countries such as Romania which was told to privatise and then sell-off its steel industry in Galati to Arcelor-Mittal before allowed becoming EU member, Ukraine will have to swallow bitter pills contained in the investment agreement championed by EIB, EBRD, IMF and World Bank.

The key issue in Ukrainian politics these days is not like in other countries where the opposition challenges the government but it is rather a fight between two oligarch-groups, namely the Kolomoysky-Group which is represented by Prime Minister Julya Tymochenko and her husband who is also very successful in the gas-business and on the other side former Prime Minister Yanukovich who was trying to sell-off the privatised Luganskteplovos group to a Russian oligarch.

To be pro-European or pro-Russian in Ukraine in these circles is rather defined these days by solid business interests, not ideological or cultural differences.

The clan of former Prime Minister Yanukovich planned to sell some 500 formerly state-controlled companies to Russian oriented oligarchs such as Rinat Achmetov, the "richest man of Ukraine".

Here, the Kolomoysky – Tymochenko Clan interfered and demanded from President Yushchenko to allow them to give the EU what Western European conglomerates may think should be theirs.

The frequently repeating gas- dispute with Russia is only one facette over which Russia and the West are sparring.

DALAI LAMA AND OTHER MODERN FEUDALISTIC CLERICS

It neither needs an Ayatollah nor any religious fanatics sponsored by a Washington based private international security firm, Harbour Lane Associates, which among former CIA boss and Ex-President George Herbert Walker Bush and former Pentagon chief William Cohen also lists John Ackerly, who Reuters quoted as major source for the "International Campaign for Tibet" on 15th March 2008, a former agent undermining in close cooperation with State Department and CIA Eastern European Stalinist dictatorships and who now represents His Holiness the Dalai Lama in order to create a minority problem.

A book titled "The CIA's Secret War in Tibet" was published in 2002 by the University Press of Kansas. The two authors - Kenneth Conboy of the Heritage Foundation and James Morrison, an Army veteran trainer for the CIA - proudly detail how the CIA set up and ran Tibet's so-called resistance movement. It is also quite remarkable that the Western free World supports a movement that in their belief and in practise treats women less respectful than women in the Afghanistan of the Taliban or Khomeini's Iran are treated by advocating sexual exploitation and a demeanour way that clearly contradicts any human rights standards we are usually quick to defend by throwing bombs. It shows what geopolitics is about: strategic advantages. If we can destabilize China by supporting the Tibetans we align ourselves quickly with people whose aims are feudalistic and clearly directed against emancipation of women. But in Afghanistan and Iran where it suits for laying pipelines or getting access to oil resources we find it easy to tell our citizens that we protect human rights. Europe and the US are speaking with a split tongue.

Europe, lacking any fanatic spiritual leaders, manages to fuel nationalism and chauvinism all on it's own. Of course, such strives for 'independence' of ethnic groups who could barely survive on their own in real terms consist of economic reasons. The standoff between China and the West with the Tibetans who were trying to snuff-out the Olympic flame should also be seen in the light of major powers trying to get a foot into the door of the resource-rich province. The Dalai Lama's response to my question doesn't deny the fact that his campaign can be linked to the Washington based security firm. His answer to my question whether it wasn't counterproductive for his campaign doesn't imply the allegations weren't true, so in this sense his reply was quite funny.

Also quite remarkable that His Holiness noted later in the press conference that China was not a Marxist socialist state but a capitalistic one. Well, this may explain why the Dalai Lama is no longer seeking independence but only autonomy as a feudal – religious regime he and his followers seem to be eager to erect could hardly be seen as a contradiction to a capitalistic system, wouldn't it?

THE HOLY GERMAN EMPIRE OF EUROPEAN NATIONS

A similar article has been published in a previous book[31]. The present situation in the EU makes it appear right to up-date and re-publish it.

The European Union is dominated by Germany. It's economic power has expanded ever since and while the EU's expansion towards the East has predominantly benefited German industries the introduction of the Euro likewise has cemented Germany's influence in the Western European nations.

A bit cynically one could say that Germany finally has succeeded by economic means where Hitler's terrorism of Nazi-Germany has failed six decades ago. Nevertheless, Germany seems to follow the principles of the *Third Reich* as it still trying to develop a pan-European hegemony that shuns France and Great-Britain while playing on the flute of nationalism and racism that had led into disaster for two times in the 20th century. The Lisbon-treaty had been the latest of the milestones Germany had tried to impose but the financial crisis got into Berlin's way.

The government of the Federal Republic of Germany continuously paid about 140 Million German Marks on an annual basis for

---

31 "Waiting for the new Führer" by Ralph T. Niemeyer (2003)

"supporting German Minorities in East, 'Central' and Southeast Europe". In 1995 it has been 143 million DM. Through the following years it has been 140 million.[32]

At least 110 million DM were spent on "Direct support for the German 'minorities' and their abilities to make a living abroad". This describes acts of sovereignty which Germany again executed outside its own borders. The funds were spent on "administrative units in territories occupied by German nationals".

The fact that those territories were parts of neighbouring states, whose inhabitants, citizens respectively, can not legally be governed by German authorities, seemed not to disturb anybody. Due to the minister of the interior's never-changed blood line principle definition, people are German if they have a certain proof of ancestry. That's why the German budget reserved such funds to be paid "for German-occupied regions or future regions to be occupied by Germans." Indeed, this follows the ancient NAZI policy and ideology, and the German government not only did not distance itself from such heritage but even enforced it in the Kosovo-Albanian conflict in Yugoslavia.

The war was meant to show the good German attitude to fight for minority rights and human rights of others in order to be able to demand the same in future conflicts where populations of German origin were affected, i.e. in the former Soviet Union or France, Belgium, Austria and Italy or Poland.

Relevant funds are channelled through an organization known as BdN[33] to FUEV[34], which calls itself in English, 'Federation of independent European Nationalities'. This does not quite meet the exact translation nor does it reflect the meaning of the German term "Volksgruppen".

The U.S. State Department wrote with good reason in 1943: "The 'Volk' (as the Germans again are defining it) is an obscure, compelling, natural entity, bound together by blood and common culture. It is entirely different from our notion of 'people', the social community

---

32 Bundeshaushalt 1997 (federal budget), BMI (Ministry of the Interior), Kapitel 0640, page 376.

33 Bund deutscher Nordschleswiger/Federation of German North Schleswig people

34 Föderation Europäischer Volksgruppen/Federation of European Folk Groups (bloodline principle)

of citizens having an open, conscious, and optional allegiance to a political union of their own making. The 'Volk' is rather conceived, on the one hand, as a natural organism and as such exerting a compulsory hold on the individual through blood relationship and, on the other hand, as a supranational being, imposing an absolute claim for loyalty and allegiance."[35]

The Federation of European Nationalities (Folk groups) is nothing else than an ancient German foreign policy tool, an organisation reflecting the NAZI policies of the twenties and thirties of the twentieth century, following the ideology of racists. Their aim was to let it supersede by a so-called European Centre of Minorities (ECM) which sounds much more civil.

In fact, the FUEV support meant to employ the racist and fascist policy of the dark German past. And, indeed, at that time German chancellor Gerhard Schröder's claim for 'continuity' is also reflected in saying that "Germany calls itself a Great Power" again,[36] as well as former Chancellor Helmut Kohl's presumption that "Germany has concluded from its history that it may now openly demand a leading role in world policy."[37]

Schröder, as well as previously Kohl, supported FUEV by state funding, although this organisation had its roots in NAZI organizations. And whereas the authors of said State Department memorandum emphasised the blood line principle of the term "VOLK," they described accurately the racist meaning of such and reflected these in the terms racial or folk community as well as racial corpus.

According to its own publications (article 3 of the memorandum), FUEV demands the creation of an internationally recognised "Volksgruppenrecht", a right for folk groups and minorities, and it even refers in its own statements to the well-known minority-groups of the thirties of the last century. Moreover, it claims to be the legal

---

35 Special Unit of the Division of European Affairs, Washington, 1943. Seite 67, Raymond Murphy, National Socialism.

36 International Herald Tribune 13 September 1999

37 „Deutschland hat mit seiner Geschichte abgeschlossen, es kann sich künftig offen zu seiner Weltmachtrolle bekennen und soll diese ausweiten." Dr. Helmut Kohl, chancellor, original quotation of statement made in the German Bundestag file No. 29287/1991.

representative and heir of such groups whose links with the NAZI government is historically evident.[38]

The magazine of this particular institution, "Nation & Staat" (Nation and State) in 1932 (publishing year six), dealt with the segregation of Jews, while the magazine of the FUEV, "Europa Ethnica", published in it's 18th year in 1961 (!!) even publicly states on its front page that it stands in the tradition of the NAZI paper "Nation & State". It advanced to become the most prominent paper for organisations like "Union of German hood Abroad"[39] (Verein für das Deutschtum im Ausland VDA, Bonn), "Hermann-Niermann-Stiftung", Düsseldorf, as well as "Federation of German North Schleswig people" (Bund deutscher Nordschleswiger BdN und FUEV). The paper received annually 10 million marks official support from the federal government, channelled through "Hermann-Niermann-Stiftung". Enormous funds were used for the support of a European Minority and Folk group initiative, basically demanding independence for minorities in regions of special interest like Scotland, Wales, Northern Ireland, Alsace, Corsica, Macedonia, Greece, Kosovo, Cataluna, Czech Republic, Eupen-Malmedy (Belgium), Southern Tyrol, Northern Italy (Padania, Veneto), Basque region, Dutch Friesland, Bretonia, Finland (Samen and Lappen), Kaliningrad (Russia), Romania, Chechnya, and so on.[40]

The German media reflected proudly that the "ethnic principle of minority and folk group protection can be successfully implemented, not only in Europe but also in Asia."[41]

In order to find a way to Europeanize the method of disintegration, and let it appear independent and worthy of support as it claims to be, multinational, European and helping to overcome the division of the European continent and its nations as every European Institution for a while had a positive image, the European Centre for Minorities indeed developed an image of a caring institution understanding and supporting the minorities in a good way.

---

38 „Information. Föderalistische Union Europäischer Volksgruppen", Generalsekretariat, Flensburg, page 4

39 Verein für das Deutschtum im Ausland

40 Budget of the Federal Government, page 379/ Bundeshaushalt 1997, Seite 379

41 FAZ 13 February 1998

In fact, the ECM (European Centre for Minorities) issues have been founded largely by those German organisations which don't even try to hide their roots in the "Third Reich".

Documents from the Ministry of the Interior make it clear that FUEV had to play a key role in the foundation of the ECM, [42] and as the headquarters of the ECM are in walking distance from the FUEV office in Apenrade, Schleswig Holstein, there have been intensive synergy effects. Moreover, at that time German foreign minister Klaus Kinkel on 2nd May 1995 wrote that the ECM operations shall be effectively coordinated through the Foreign Office, department VI and department KII5 of the Ministry of the Interior.[43]

And the Social Democratic-Green coalition government of Chancellor Gerhard Schröder and Foreign Minister Joseph ("Joschka") Fischer not only did not stop such illegal activities, but even encouraged them and used the ethnic principle the first time after WWII again when claiming to protect ethnic minorities in Yugoslavia. They just fell short of the logical-sounding propaganda of Adolf Hitler when rushing to "defend" German minorities in the Czech Republic of those days. How powerful these groups were one could see when it came to Yugoslavia. The ground has been prepared to "defend minorities" and their drive for independence.

Nowadays, as the focus in the EU is moving back from Brussels to the various member state governments and the national level, we might see an ever more intense campaign for "independence" of ethnic minorities and autonomy of regions in various countries. The idea of a *Europe of the Regions* has been invented in Germany but it affects almost all nation states except for Germany itself. But, beneficiaries of nationalistic movements seeking to split up nation states such as Belgium, Spain or Great-Britain are also to be found within those countries: it is in the interest of major industries and multinational corporations to see centralised power be split up as it becomes easier to

---

42 Documents of the Interior Ministry BMI Dokument für Gründung Europäischen Minderheitenzentrums, 15 October 1993

43 Foreign Minister Klaus Kinkel wrote in a letter dated 02 May 1995 to a MP that the ECM's cross border activities shall be conducted by Department VI of the Foreign Ministry as well as Dept. KII5 of the Interior Ministry.

play one constituency against the other and blackmail elected councils, ethnic 'parliaments'. This may result in a tax dumping competition between Flanders and Wallonie, Scotland, England and Wales, Bask, Catalan, Alsace, Südtirol and Padania, Regio Veneto and Sicilia and so on.

Meanwhile, Germany will stand tall and strong in the centre of Europe having degraded all of it's neighbours who will dance to the tune of the German Bundesbank and European Central Bank in Frankfurt.

VIII.

If God asked whether you're good for a loan, were you?!

BLACK FRIGHT-DAY

(by R.Nie "Ernie")

It was a on a Friday afternoon that I had a nap after eating a delicious Spaghetti Bolognaise for lunch. I dreamed I was sleeping when the bloody telephone rang.

It was God, the King.

"Are you good for a loan, Ernie" the Almighty asked with a hollow sound in his voice as one would expect it when being connected directly to heaven.

I felt that the blood was leaving my brain.

"I am not sure" I uttered as neither my brain nor my voice was functioning well.

"What do you mean, is that a 'yeah' or 'nay' Ernie?"

I quickly went through my personal finances. I still got a 50 € note from my September pocket money my wife gave me and the Octo-Bear was already lingering around the corner, so I could afford a loan, but why would The Lord ask someone like me for that? Was it really that bad already?! Also, did I smell a hoax here? I hadn't heard from God for all my life so it was a bit awkward that he rang me totally out of the blue, so to say.

"I could," I replied after a brief moment "but how can I lend money to someone I don't know?"

The silence in the phone line that followed could not be overheard. It dawned at me that it could be seen as impolite to say that I didn't know God, so what could I do to limit the damage?

"You don't believe in Me, Ernie?" God asked with a certain tremble in his voice that let me shiver.

"Uh no, I mean, yes, yes Your Lordship, I do believe in You!" I was quick to assure Him.

"I am not a Lordship, I am Your Lord, Ernie."

"Ah, yes, My Lord, I forgot."

"You forgot, Ernie?! I am your creator."

"No My Creator, don't worry, I would never forget You. How could I?!"

"Good, so let's talk about the loan."

"The loan? How come My Lord is asking me, the poor old Ernie, for that, are things that bad?"

"There is recession up here, too, Ernie, and the Holy Sea spoilt it for us by issuing the new mortal sins."

"Mortal sins?!" I stupidly asked as I had forgotten for a brief moment who I was talking to.

"Don't tell Me that you don't know about the 7 mortal sins, Ernie!" God, the King, said with a sharp tone in his voice.

"Almighty, I know about the ten commandments, such as don't covet your neighbour's wife, his ox or donkey, or don't kill a false witness or steal a cast idol and make no wrongful use of Your name" I recalled as good as I could.

"And", God the King went on "The firstborn of a donkey you shall redeem with a lamb, or if you will not redeem it you shall break it's neck. All the firstborn of your sons you shall redeem. No one shall appear before Me empty-handed. The best of the first fruits of your ground you shall bring to the house of the Lord your God."

"I would, My Almighty, but I don't have a penny to my knee. Why is it, that, if the Ten Commandments are still valid, would you have to ask for a loan?" I asked but the deep sounding voice of God lectured me that because the Vatican under Papa Razzi had declared excessive wealth a mortal sin and following this new principle cardinals were seen throwing money through the windows of St. Peter's Sistine chapel.

"You see" God the king concluded "we got a crisis up here as well."

"I see, Almighty, I can give you all of what is left over from my September pocket money, but I strongly suggest that you send your best man down to us to straighten things out otherwise we will never get out of the mess." I said.

"Very good, we shall do so." God the king replied.

Then, He passed on the phone to His son. He listened to the unique name of Jesus Christ.

"Hello?" the Son of God said.

"Hello!" I confirmed as I was not sure how to address the Son of God

"Who is it?"

"It's me, Ernie."

"From where are you calling?"

"I didn't call, your dad rang me up. I am on Earth, the planet next to Mars."

"I see. He is doing that with many people right now."

"Seems there is a bit of trouble everywhere right now, especially on Earth" I explained.

"Yeah, I have been there once a little while ago" the Son of God replied suppressing a yawning.

"That has been 2000 years ago! Wouldn't it be good to pay us a visit again" I insisted.

"Oh yes, you are right, let me look into that. What about Wednesday?

Next Wednesday came and I was poised to go to Shannon airport to collect the Son of God, but he had not given me any specific time or any other instructions. Then again, who knows how the top management of heaven travelled? Certainly not the way the CEOs of the American car industry travelled to Washington DC when they were summoned by Congress last year. Maybe the Son of God came by elves or reindeers, uh no that was Father Christmas, I recon. I got a bit excited as I couldn't imagine how it would be to meet the Son of God.

I did not have to drive all the way to Shannon airport as the Son of God suddenly stood in my garden on Wednesday morning when I came back from jogging with Schlumpy, the best, most beautiful, only dog I have. I immediately recognised the Son of God as he looked exactly as I had thought he would look, long hair, long beard, dressed in kind of a long white night gown wearing sandals on our planet, Earth, only Jesus-freaks would wear.

"Hi" said the Son of God as he came closer and offered me his hand which I shook as my senses slowly came back to me.

"Hello My Lord" I replied but the Son of God only shook his head "My friends call me Jesus." He said.

"I am honoured" I replied and offered Him a chair but He sat down on the grass so I sat next to Him.

"So what's the matter, Ernie?" He asked looking with his beautiful eyes at me.

"Everything is out of control, Jesus. We don't know how to cope with the crisis. Shops are closing down, people loose their work, the elderly don't get proper treatment in hospitals anymore, our kids have no school-books anymore, theatres and concert halls are closed, and our governments tell us to tighten our belts." I explained.

The Son of God stared at the lake in front of us. Is it true, that he once walked on water and over a lake I wondered and promised to myself to ask Him later. It would be great for Schlumpy and me to be able to take a shortcut across the Shannon river to Mountshannon where we always wanted to jog to. And, was it that if one could walk on water, that one could also jog over it? I banned those thoughts from my brain for a while as we had more pressing issues to discuss.

"That has always been like that, even the last time I have been here" Jesus interrupted my childish thinking. Then he turned towards me.

"Show me around." He said and stood up. I took him by his arm and led him onto the road. We walked a bit before we came to a new house. "You see, we have many of these new houses now. For the past ten years we built houses over houses and sold them for a lot of money" I explained "Each house was financed by more than 120% so that a young couple could have even the wedding ceremony, a car or two cars, the furniture and their honeymoon, but then they had to pay it back over the next 30 years. At the same time prices for bred and vegetables were rising. Now, nobody is able to afford the houses anymore but because we have now 2 houses per family the prices are falling. Nobody wants to buy more houses and people fear that they loose their work and then can't stay in their house anymore."

Jesus looked at a new bungalow we stood in front. Then he said: "It is because your economy only produces for profit and not actual needs.

That's why your industries produce such an incredible amount of trash. Only what gives a good return on investment is deemed necessary to be produced even if nobody really wants those products." Jesus said and I nodded. "Well, here in Europe we at least built the houses we talked about but in America they only showed growth rates in the real estate market but built less houses than 40 years ago. They just made us believe that because the houses being built ten years ago were better than those being built 40 years ago. And relative to the income a house cost much more than the decades before. The same happened with the cars manufacturing industry. They produced and sold less cars than in the decades before but nevertheless were able to show growth rates in that sector because of quality adjustments in statistics. Of course technology had advanced and made cars nowadays be better than 30 years ago but they have also become much more expensice relative to the income" I explained and the Son of God looked very serious before He spoke again.

"You shouldn't drive around in cars that much anyhow. But the real problem is that someone has taken advantage of people believing in these manipulations. Mankind should be in a position to produce better and more quality goods in an ecological way preserving nature and evolution." He replied striving over his long beard. "But how?", I asked. "These people have become so enormously rich and have all the power to dictate our politicians what they want in order to maximize their profit. Six of the world's major 10 corporations are energy conglomerates who hardly have any interest in producing less emission" I told the Son of God. "They are talking on their TV channels and in their media about fighting 'Climate Change' and tell us that we shall fuel our cars with 'bio-fuel' while at the same time half of the world's population is under-nourished. We could grow edibles on the same land, but they tell us that the penguins are worried about icebergs being cried by the glaciers into the oceans. They say that one could grow broccoli in the valley from which the glaciers had retracted but I am afraid penguins don't like broccoli." I said and Jesus looked at me in disbelief.

"Climate Change is a serious issue and you are right, there are interest groups that jump onto the bandwagon. It is because one allows these groups to set the agenda and favour the wrong priorities under a false pretence" the Son of God after a brief moment of silence said.

189

"And, the same people tell us that nuclear power was emission-free and would save the planet from being overheated" I continued "and keep the poles from melting, but it could as well be that we have managed to blow up the planet well before the change in climate has wiped out life on Earth. On top of that we still have no solution for the nuclear waste. They told us 40 years ago that it was safe to seal it in containers and put it into tunnels but now we find that these containers are leaking and contaminate the soil. We could as well wrap the nuclear waste in plastic bags and dump it in a school yard so that our children and grandchildren can get acquainted with it as they will have to deal with it anyways."

Jesus' face carried an ever more worrisome expression as he probably thought carefully about what I told him. "So while the Climate Change hype of our media seems to have led to a revival of nuclear energy one forgot about the penguins. Instead of reverting to alternative energy concepts which existed for many years already the investment funds are creating another bubble getting us ever deeper into trouble. The day will come that we will have to pay back and then they will tell us that unfortunately they have lost all the money because of 'bad market' but in reality someone will have stolen it from us." I complained.

"That's why you should ban all speculation to the casinos. Let people gamble there if they have fun with it. In economic decisions one is tempted to be led by randomly selected numbers like in a casino like in the ancient Greek society when the oracle made the decisions.

But don't let them dominate your lives. It is far too important not to take serious decisions in one's own hands. Money used for speculations can be replaced with tokens for the casinos. Then it wouldn't have any negative effect if these people miss-speculated. Mankind should take it's own fate into it's own hands. Decisions shall not be made by corrupt structures such as those political parties that have been bribed by the economic powerful but by those who are really affected by those decisions. They shall decide on a democratic basis. That's what we tried to do last time I was here" Jesus replied. I thought about it for a moment. "But" I asked "it didn't work out well in the end, didn't it? Someone sold his soul by giving your name to the persecutors for a few silver coins and you got crucified. How could we make sure that wouldn't happen again?!"

The Son of God raised his eyebrows. "You remember that?"

"Well, it was written about it all along, one could hardly not know about it. The Holy Catholic church made a lot of money with selling Your story" I commented.

"I see, but I never had authorised them to speak in my name. You see it had been better we had abolished money right then and there. We wouldn't have had any trouble, then." Jesus replied.

I was fascinated. "How would that work? I mean how can we make sure our economies aren't running low on liquidity to produce? The standard of living for the masses is declining since decades, the food we eat is more unhealthy than ever before, the water we drink is poisoned, our entertainers and football stars earn more than our scientists. Our concert halls and theatres are closed, the musicians of our times play Beethoven as if they were on the run from the composer, our architecture won't be there in a hundred years anymore, our literature, our art, I doubt that anyone will look at it in the future. More has been left over from Cesar's time than from the 20th century. And the reason for that is, one hears all along, that we don't have enough money. On the other hand we are being told that per capita we become richer than ever before which doesn't mean that we equally become richer. Just a few of us, and now You tell me that we should abolish money?! It would be a dream that no Jedi Riders had a grip on our economies anymore but I can't believe it" I got enraged but the Son of God had a mild expression on his face showing all the mercy and clemency we humans can receive.

"Yes, that indeed would be the solution. You see, the countries that have been deprived of their rights for so long and got indebted with the rich countries have paid back what is deemed their debt a long time ago already but they are still indebted with the industrialised world, so why is there starvation?" the Son of God hypothetically asked "Yes, I should have done something about it but I saw that productivity was rising faster than the world's population so in that sense I thought there wouldn't be any problem, it is rather the distribution of wealth that poses as a problem."

Here I felt I had to intervene. We had poor people in the so called 'first world', too.

"And what is granny doing? She is poor, too, but lives in an industrialised country." I asked a bit provokingly.

"Why?" Jesus asked.

"Her pension is too little."

"But if you became richer on a per capita basis than ever before it should be equal whether a capita is 8, 18 or 80 years old it means that there is ever more that could be shared, wouldn't it?"

"Yes."

"So again it is a mere question of distribution of wealth. Productivity was rising constantly while the standard of living is declining. A rise in productivity means that one can produce high quality products by using less labour and even opens possibilities for requiring less energy. There shouldn't be a problem in supplying everyone with good, healthy food and durable high quality goods" said Jesus.

"But one would also need more capital." I replied but the Son of God shrug his shoulders indicating that this was unimportant.

"The substance of capital are machines, know how and technology and that again is the result of labour" the Son of God explained "the problem you mention of capital supply for production is a problem which only exists in the profit orientated financial capitalism. If there was no money one wouldn't have any of these problems. Today, money is only invested when it multiplies and where it makes the biggest profit regardless of what is actually needed." Jesus emphasised.

"Yes, and marketing specialists try to make us believe then that we actually want all that but at the same time all goods we actually want aren't there in sufficient quantity. Instead, they produce all this trash that dissolves so quickly. The fashion we have is like uniforms but they try to sell it to us as *individuality* but that individuality is coming by bulk! If productivity is rising we in fact should be richer than before." I concluded.

"No, don't say 'rich' anymore. All money shall be abolished. It will be replaced by time", God's first born son proposed "then nobody can horde time like they did it with money but everyone will have good quality products and enough to eat and drink and will have healthcare and being taken care of when being old."

I was not really satisfied, yet.

"But can everyone afford it?" I asked.

"Well, we have time. It is not the question anymore whether it is financially affordable, but *timely* affordable instead" the Son of God explained.

"I can't follow" I admitted. Jesus sat down on a stone and pointed at another one where I should sit down too. So I did.

"What else is money if not the reflection of what can be produced within a certain time?" he asked and looked with his vivid eyes directly into mine.

"High productivity means that one can not only produce high quality goods for a few but for everyone" Jesus said "I can't understand why you're producing so much trash although you got the ability to produce environmentally good quality in high quantity?"

I gave it a thought. "But who decides what is being produced?" I asked.

"The very person that actually wants to use the product. In the future one won't order pre-produced trash but individually self-designed good quality products of which there will be more than plenty. Then a changing fashion doesn't make sense anymore as everyone can decide himself what he or she wants and order exactly that."

"That sounds too good to be true" I criticised but Jesus shook his head.

"It is not. Just the way production is organised today is not wise at all. It is anti-economical and also against the environment and against evolution. The last time I have been on Earth a farmer would work on the field of an aristocrat all day but same aristocrat would not tell the farmers working on his fields that not enough had been harvested to feed them, but exactly that is the case nowadays when the average people are denied their share in the accumulated wealth. If the owner of a factory tells his workers that there was not enough that has been produced, why should they believe it? God wants us to put the priorities right and protect evolution, all species, Earth. Today, your society claims to be free. More advanced than people in medieval times but for many today *Freedom* is only a tag because people are in many ways not more free than a thousand years ago."

"But how shall we live together? Who shall make the decisions?" I curiously asked.

"By democracy. People will form ad-hoc committees and share their interests and work together to achieve a goal.

You know, the Latin word *privare* also means *to rob*. Privatizations have robbed people of everything. You have to put it under control of the people who are affected by it."

"But how do we fight corruption?"

"By democratic control mechanisms. There will be less Corruption if there are enough goods for all and if the currency is not money but time. It doesn't make sense anymore to take advantage of a situation if there is a fair distribution of wealth."

"And the inefficiencies?" I asked.

"Very simple, those who are more efficient and do their work better can have more time." Jesus replied.

"But time for what?"

"To do whatever they like."

"Also build another house?"

"If they want...but what would they want the second house for?"

"To rent it out."

"That won't be possible as one can only be paid in time not money or goods. And you see even those who under present conditions have two or more houses can't make use of it although money still exists. It only causes trouble" the Son of God said and I couldn't deny Him some logic in his argument.

"Trouble...trouble" I murmured. I wanted to say something else but I couldn't formulate it. The sentences were somewhere in my head and a few words made it down to my tongue but somehow they couldn't get out...and across the lips.

If money will be abolished, hey how do I get my 50€ I extended as a loan to God the King back? I wondered, still thinking in my little greedy way....

Then my wife entered the room.

"Who were you talking to?" she asked.

"Godseckin" I uttered turned over to try to fall asleep again and re-enter my dream otherwise, how would I ever get my 50 € back? And, what about interest? Ouch, not a good one, interest was prohibited by the Old Testament! Then, I woke up from my beautiful dream during an afternoon nap on a Friday during the height of the financial crisis and I wished I had slept through the entire crisis.

PS: This planet has not been a gift, it rather is a loan.

I don't want to be the one who has to explain to the owner why it has been run down so badly.